# STEEL RAIN

## Waffen-SS Panzer Battles in the West 1944–1945

Tim Ripley

MBI Publishing Company

This edition first published in 2001 by MBI Publishing Company,
Galtier Plaza, Suite 200, 380 Jackson Street, St. Paul, MN 55101-3885

MBI Publishing Company books are also available at discounts in bulk quantity
for industrial or sales-promotional use. For details write to Special Sales Manager
at Motorbooks International Wholesalers & Distributors, Galtier Plaza, Suite 200,
380 Jackson Street, St. Paul, MN 55101-3885.

Library of Congress Cataloging-in-Publication Data Available.

ISBN 0-7603-1168-4

Printed in Hong Kong

For Brown Partworks Limited
8 Chapel Place
Rivington Street
London
EC2A 3DQ

Editors: Peter Darman, Vanessa Unwin
Picture research: Antony Shaw
Design: Stefan Podhorodecki, Iain Stuart
Maps: Bob Garwood
Production: Matt Weyland

# CONTENTS

# CONTENTS

# DEDICATION AND ACKNOWLEDGEMENTS

*Dedication*

This book is dedicated to the heroes of the US Army's 291st Engineer Combat Battalion, who at the moment of crisis blew the strategic bridges on 18 December 1944 to stop the advance of SS-Obersturmbannführer Jochen Peiper's Kampfgruppe at the height of the Battle of the Bulge. Men like Corporal Fred Chaplin, who pushed the plunger to blow the bridge at Habiemont as Peiper's tanks bore down on him, were in the vanguard of turning back Hitler's Waffen-SS panzer élite, so freeing Europe of Nazi tyranny for good.

*Acknowledgements*

The author would like to thank the following for their help during the researching and writing of this study: Neil Tweedie and Micky Brooks for their assistance in providing an understanding World War II Blitzkrieg strategy; the records staff of the Imperial War Museum in London for their help with research into German World War II documents; the British Army Staff College, Camberley, for allowing me access to rare German World War II records in their possession; Stewart Fraser for proof-reading my text; Pete Darman, of Brown Partworks, for at last giving me the opportunity to fulfil my long-held ambition to write about the Waffen-SS; and, last but not least, Major Hasse Resenbro of the Danish Guard Hussar Regiment for his help retracing the escape route of Kampfgruppe *Peiper* from La Gleize.

# Key to Maps

## Military units – types

☒ infantry

▬ armoured

▱ motorized infantry/ panzergrenadier

⛉ parachute/airborne

## Military units – size

XXXXX army group

XXXX army

XXX corps

XX division

X brigade

III regiment

II battalion

## Military unit colours

German

British and Commonwealth

US

## Military movement

atttack/advance (in national colours)

## Geographical symbols

road

• urban area

urban area

trees

track

marsh

river

railway

bridge

# List of Maps

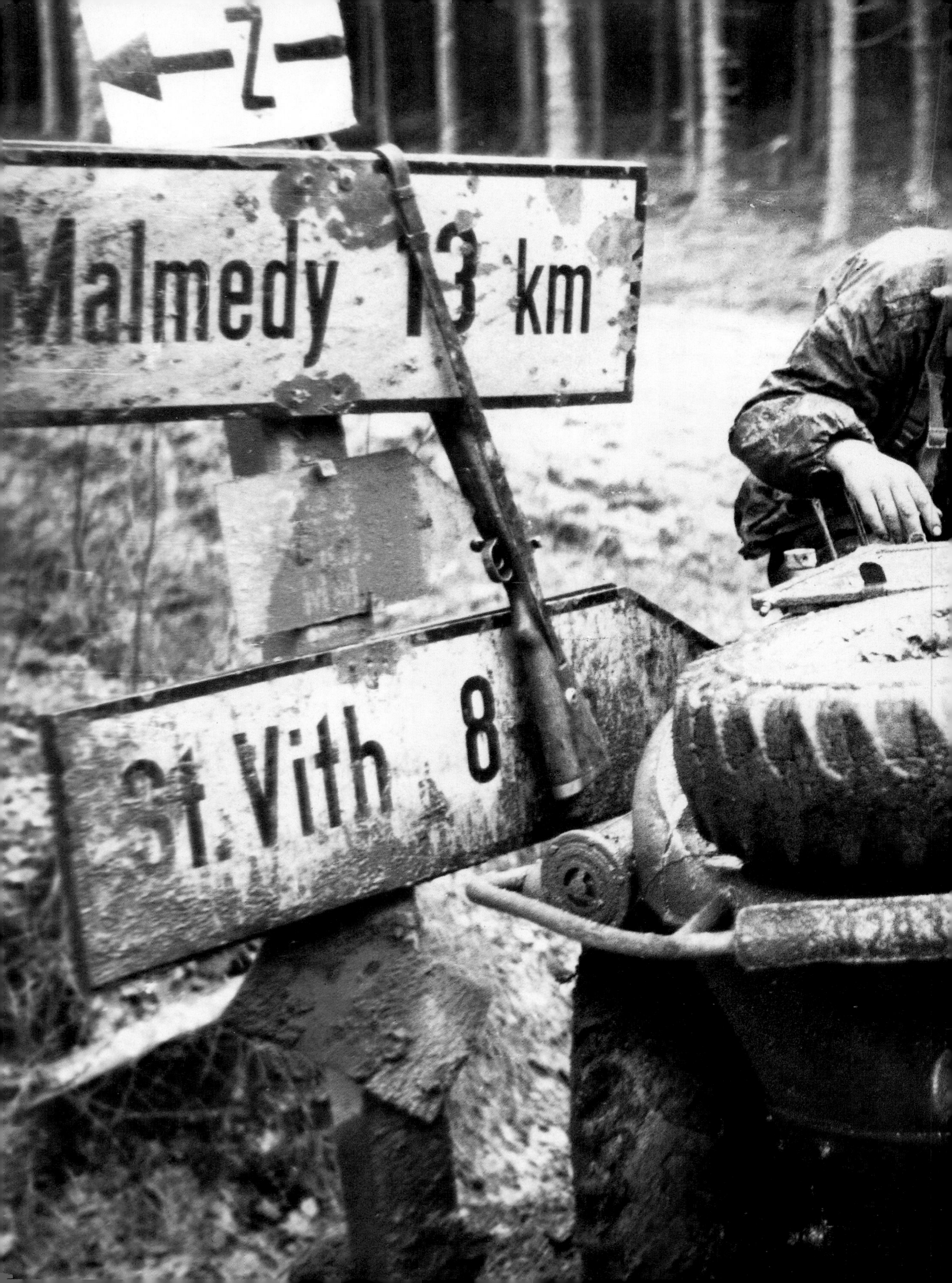
Z
Malmedy 13 km
St. Vith 8

# CHAPTER 1

# BATTLE GROUP *PEIPER*

## The failure of a desperate gamble in December 1944.

Christmas morning 1944. Just under 800 cold and half-starved Waffen-SS men emerged from the morning gloom to pass through the frontline German trenches to safety. At their head was the charismatic 29-year-old SS-Oberstürmbannführer Jochen Peiper, who had led them for almost two days through thick woods, pursued by American patrols and spotter planes. The Waffen-SS officer was still joking with his men, slapping their backs and encouraging them to keep moving.

Only eight days before, Peiper had led a Kampfgruppe (battle group) of some 5800 men forward into battle. They had at first swept all before them, penetrating deep behind enemy lines, before their luck and petrol had started to run out. Captured American petrol dumps kept Peiper's 100 Tiger II, Panther and Panzer IV tanks moving for the first few days of Operation Autumn Mist, as the Ardennes Offensive had been codenamed by Hitler. In the heady days of the advance, the Kampfgruppe ensured its eternal notoriety when it machine-gunned a group of unarmed US Army prisoners of war in a field outside the town of Malmédy.

Peiper drove his men hard. He was often seen at the head of his huge column of tanks and vehicles, sorting out traffic jams, or

■ *Left:* Near Malmédy – the Belgian town where Jochen Peiper's troops machine-gunned unarmed US prisoners of war in a field.

■ *Above: At 29 years of age at the end of 1944, Peiper was the archetypal Waffen-SS officer. He rose to the top after a series of stunning battlefield performances on the Eastern Front, where this photograph of him was taken.*

bridges and supply dumps with ease. One US general was just able to flee his command post less than half an hour before the arrival of Peiper's panzers, much to his chagrin.

As the Americans regained their composure, they started to rebuild their defences. Time and again, Peiper's men found their route blocked by dug-in and determined defenders. On three occasions, for example, the Americans managed to blow up a vital bridge just as a group of Waffen-SS panzers was coming into view. Slowly Peiper found his options being closed down, one by one.

## On the defensive

A week into the advance, Kampfgruppe *Peiper* was badly battered by almost constant fighting. Its ammunition and fuel was nearly exhausted. The 1000 or so men still capable of fighting had not eaten a proper cooked meal since they had left Germany on 16 December, at the start of the attack. Peiper realized his attack had run out of momentum and started to pull his men back to the hilltop village of La Gleize to make a last stand. American tank columns were pushing against his force from the west, north and east. The Luftwaffe attempted to make a supply drop to the beleaguered Waffen-SS men, but most of the containers of ammunition and petrol ended up behind American lines. Peiper repeatedly radioed his divisional commander, SS-Oberführer Wilhelm Mohnke, asking for permission to break out.

La Gleize had been turned into a fortified strongpoint by Peiper's men. Tiger II tanks with massive 88mm cannons blocked all the approach routes, making it impossible for the lightly armoured US Shermans to get through. Waffen-SS panzergrenadiers

exhorting them to attack yet another American position blocking their route to the River Meuse, the 1st SS Panzer Division *Leibstandarte Adolf Hitler*'s objective.

Heavy mist, snow slurries and incessant rain kept the Allied fighter-bomber squadrons at bay most of the time, but it made life miserable for the Waffen-SS men, shivering in their freezing tanks or open SdKfz 251 armoured halftracks. Few men got any sleep as the column weaved its way along single track roads and around hairpin bends. The key to victory was the handful of bridges that crossed the swollen rivers of the Ardennes.

The bad weather and the element of surprise worked in Peiper's favour for the first couple of days. They stormed past confused and disorganized American troops, capturing

*Time and again, Peiper's men found their route blocked by dug-in and determined defenders*

were posted in the woods around the town to stop US infantrymen infiltrating. Attack after attack was repulsed with heavy American losses. The solid Belgian houses of the village made safe havens from the almost hourly American artillery bombardments that were raining down on La Gleize. Hundreds of captured Americans were hiding in the cellars, alongside the steadily

increasing numbers of German wounded. Peiper was often seen touring the improvised field hospitals to raise morale among "his boys". The English-speaking Waffen-SS officer struck up a rapport with a senior American prisoner, Major Hal McCowan. Even as he was planning the escape of his decimated Kampfgruppe, Peiper was still maintaining to McCowan that Germany was winning the war and that the Führer's new secret V-weapons would turn the tide of the conflict in the Third Reich's favour.

On the evening of 23 December, Peiper was finally given permission to break out from La Gleize. He convened a swift meeting of his senior commanders. There was no way to get any of the Kampfgruppe tanks or vehicles past American lines, so the breakout would have to be made on foot. Anyway, there was no fuel left. The wounded would be left behind and tasked with destroying the undamaged tanks, artillery pieces and half-tracks. This was not to begin until Peiper and the main body of men were safely away from the village, so as not to alert the Americans that the breakout was under way. By 02:00 hours everything was ready. Peiper was still outwardly confident, and even made

**■ *Above:* The remnants of Peiper's battle group hid in the woods covering the Mont St Victor hill feature for two bitterly cold nights with no food, while being hunted by American patrols.**

**■ *Left:* Kampfgruppe *Peiper* left behind 25 tanks and 50 other vehicles in La Gleize. This Tiger II is preserved outside the village's war museum.**

■ *Above:* The modern-day village of La Gleize is much as it was in December 1944 when Peiper and his men made their dramatic last stand, trapped by US forces advancing on three fronts.

McCowan sign an agreement that the Americans would release the wounded Germans remaining in the village, in return for the freedom of the US prisoners who were being left behind. McCowan was forced to march along with Peiper's column to ensure the Americans complied with the "agreement". To help with the navigation in the woods south of La Gleize, two unfortunate Belgian farmers were press-ganged into service as guides.

## Breakout from La Gleize

As the Germans left the village, moonlight reflected off the frost that covered the ground. The 800-strong column snaked along a sunken track southwards in silence. Peiper's first objective was the River Amblève and the cover of its heavily forested valley. After a half-hour march, the column reached the river and crossed a small road bridge in the shadow of the demolished large railway bridge. They then turned sharply southwards and started to climb up the steep sides of the heavily forested Mont St Victor feature.

By 05:00 hours they were at the top of the feature. From there, they were able to hear the first explosions below in La Gleize, as the stay-behind teams started to set off demolition charges in the 90 or so vehicles that had been left behind. This alerted the Americans that something unusual was happening, and patrols were sent forward and were soon in the centre of the town, freeing the 150 or so GIs that had been held by Peiper. Around 300 German prisoners – all wounded or medical personnel – were captured as the US troops combed the village for Peiper and his men. The only serious resistance came from a group of 50 panzergrenadiers who did not get the codeword, "Merry Christmas", to join the escape column. They fought to the last man on the outskirts of the village. US commanders then ordered up Piper Cub spotter aircraft to find their elusive foe.

Watching this activity below, Peiper decided to lay up in the huge forest during the next few hours of daylight until the next phase of his escape could unfold. He had originally intended to cross the railway bridge at the village of Coo, but from his hilltop perch, Peiper could see it had been demolished. Now his column would have to march southwards and find another crossing to get them over the River Salm. After managing to remain undiscovered until nightfall, the weary Waffen-SS grenadiers roused themselves from their uneasy sleep and prepared for one last push for freedom.

They marched on along a forest track in the darkness until an American sentry called out

*The weary Waffen-SS men roused themselves from sleep and prepared for one last push for freedom*

"Halt!". In silence, the Germans went to ground. The sentry repeated the challenge three times and got no response. Then he fired three shots. Thinking he must have been hearing ghosts, the sentry gave up on his hunt. Minutes later, whispered orders were issued for the column to turn around and move off in a new direction. Peiper's luck continued to hold as the column moved southwards again and allowed them to cross a major road undetected.

In the early hours of Christmas Day, the column ran into a large patrol from the US 82nd Airborne Division. This time the Americans were more alert and a brisk fire-fight ensured. Peiper's men dived for cover in the undergrowth and started to exchange fire. The Americans called in mortar fire. A pitched battle was the last thing the Waffen-SS commander wanted. His officers were slowly able to regain control of their men through the use of a lot of shouting. Gradually, they melted back into the woods and were able to regroup. No Americans followed up the action because word of the German escape attempt had not been passed to the 82nd Airborne Division by the units in La Gleize. In the confusion, the captured American officer, McCowan, and the Belgian guides were able to make their escape.

Now the column had only a few more kilometres to go to the outposts of their *Leibstandarte* comrades, but the men were at the limits of their mental and physical

■ *Below:* The field at Baugnez, southeast of Malmédy, where Peiper's men massacred nearly 100 US prisoners of war on 18 December 1944.

■ *Above:* Peiper led his column of 800 men in silence across the small foot bridge in the dead of night on Christmas Eve to infiltrate past American troops only a few hundred metres away.

endurance. Anything heavy, such as large packs or Panzerfaust antitank rockets, was dumped by the forest trails. The Germans scooped up handfuls of snow to try to fight off thirst. The worst danger was the effect of sleep deprivation. When the column halted, the Waffen-SS men had to physically shake many of their comrades to wake them from the deep sleep they immediately fell into when their bodies touched the ground. In spite of this, when the column reached the banks of the Salm and found there was no bridge, morale did not crack. The stronger men waded into the river to form a human chain for the remainder to pass along. By dawn, they were only a few hundred metres from German lines. A brief skirmish with

American troops ensued, but again they did not seem to know who they were fighting and did not press home their attack.

## Peiper's losses show

At 10:00 hours Peiper reported to his divisional commander that he had managed to bring out 770 men from La Gleize. In his epic 20km (12-mile) march, Peiper lost only 30 men. By force of personality alone he kept his column together and navigated it to safety. Eight days before, he had led 5800 men across the German border. While some wounded had been evacuated early in the battle, the majority fell into American hands. In total, some 5000 Waffen-SS men had been killed or captured during Peiper's

■ *Above:* **The monument to Peiper's victims at Baugnez.**

Kampfgruppe *Peiper* summed up the fate of the Waffen-SS panzer divisions in the West during the final year of the war. The Waffen-SS officers showed dynamic leadership and battlefield flair against opponents who had material superiority, but limited tactical experience. In adversity, the Waffen-SS panzer divisions showed that they could absorb staggering levels of casualties and still keep on fighting. They may have been good soldiers and commanders, but incidents such as the Malmédy massacre showed there was a dark side to the Waffen-SS. The Nazi indoctrination meant they were not just ordinary soldiers, but the élite battlefield spearhead of Hitler's murderous regime. What kept men like Jochen Peiper fighting was their faith in Hitler's racist ideology, and their belief that Germany's opponents were not up to the task of defeating the Third Reich. Peiper and his men were the guardians of evil. In the snowy valleys of the Ardennes, Peiper's faith in his leader's crazy war was tested to the full. After his escape from La Gleize, he was evacuated back to Germany, now physically and mentally exhausted. In his heart he knew Germany's days were numbered.

brief sortie against the US Army. For a few days, he had seriously unbalanced the American command in the Ardennes region, but once they brought their overwhelming firepower to bear on his small and poorly supplied Kampfgruppe, Peiper knew its days were numbered.

Immediately after the war, Peiper entered popular mythology as "GI Enemy Number One" because of the actions of his grenadiers at Malmédy. The odyssey of

■ *Right:* **By the end of December 1944, Hitler's great gamble had failed and it was now only a matter of time before the victorious Allies advanced into the heart of his "Thousand Year Reich".**

# CHAPTER 2

# WAFFEN-SS – PANZER ÉLITE

## A profile of the SS panzer divisions in 1944.

From the hedgerows of Normandy to the icy valleys of the Ardennes, the Waffen-SS panzer divisions proved to be the toughest opponents the Allied forces were to face during the final year of the war. They fought fanatically under the command of skilled and determined leaders. To the end, they simply never seemed to consider the fact that Germany losing the war was reason for them to give up fighting. This always bewildered their British and American opponents, many of whom valued human life far above victory itself.

Who were these men who continued fighting for a lost cause, in the face of overwhelming odds? To understand the Waffen-SS, observers need to go back to the roots of Adolf Hitler's National Socialist (or Nazi) Party in the 1920s and trace his rise to ultimate power in the 1930s.

### Origins

Hitler's paranoid political philosophy was born in his street-fighting days of the early 1920s. Germany was on the verge of revolution. *Coup d'etats* or putsch attempts were a regular occurrence as the country's Weimar fledgling democracy tried to cope with the after-

■ *Left:* The young tank crews of the *Hitlerjugend* Panzer Division painted their girlfriends' and mothers' names on their tanks.

■ *Above:* **Hitler at first built up the Waffen-SS to rival the Nazi Party's SA (Brownshirts) paramilitary militia (shown here), who threatened to become too independent of the Nazi hierarchy. The Führer demanded, and received, total loyalty from his SS guards.**

math of defeat in World War I. The Nazi Brownshirts, or Sturmabteilung (SA), were at the forefront of clashes with communists and the police of the Weimar Republic. When Hitler's so-called Beer Hall Putsch failed in November 1923, the future dictator became convinced that he would need a reliable élite paramilitary group at his disposal if he was ever to seize and hold power in Germany.

As Germany spiralled into depression, and mass unemployment took hold in the aftermath of the "great world depression" of 1929, Hitler saw his chance. While participating in elections that brought him to the brink of power, Hitler also began mobilizing his paramilitary forces.

Central to his strategy was a small, shadowy group of just over 100 young men known as the Stabswache *Berlin* (Headquarters Guard *Berlin*), that was part of the Nazi Schutz Staffel (Protection Squad) or the SS. Dressed in sinister black uniforms, the SS Stabswache *Berlin* appeared to the uninitiated to be little more than Hitler's bodyguards. Indeed, the unit was soon renamed SS *Leibstandarte Adolf Hitler* (Life Guard Regiment Adolf Hitler). They were, in fact, the armed élite of the Nazi Party, loyal only to Hitler.

The list of the membership of this first SS group reads like a who's who of the future Waffen-SS. It was led by one Josef "Sepp" Dietrich, Hitler's former chauffeur, who would rise to command the *Leibstandarte* Division and ultimately the Sixth SS Panzer Army. This unit would contain six Waffen-SS panzer divisions in its final days in April 1945. Many of the famous wartime Waffen-SS divisional and regimental commanders were members of this first group, and the bond they established in it served them well through the war and beyond.

Once Hitler rose to the Chancellorship in January 1933, he moved swiftly to consolidate his hold on power. One of his first acts was the violent elimination of the leadership of the SA in the famous Night of the Long Knives in June 1934. This saw the SS in the thick of the action, seizing scores of SA leaders and then executing them. Dietrich played a prominent part in this purge, overseeing the first extra-judicial killings which were to take place under Hitler's regime. From this point on, the nature of Germany changed. No longer was it a parliamentary democracy, governed by the rule of law. For the next 12 years it would be a ruthless dictatorship, with the SS acting as Hitler's killing machine.

In a matter of months, the SS grew into a form of parallel government, to ensure the Nazi Party could never be overthrown from within. The police, prison service, intelligence agencies and judiciary were all kept under close control by their SS counterparts. Soon the SS boasted hundreds of thousands of members, all working to ensure total obedience to the Führer's will.

Not surprisingly, Hitler viewed the Germany Army with great suspicion. It alone seemed to possess the wherewithal to remove the Nazi regime from power. Adolf Hitler, the former "Bohemian corporal", had little time for the aristocratic professional officer corps of the Germany Army, who he blamed for Germany's defeat in World War I, and immediately set about neutralizing the political power of the General Staff. He made every German soldier swear a personal oath of loyalty to him. Troublesome senior commanders were removed after trumped-up sex scandals, and others were bought off with gifts of huge estates.

> *The SS boasted hundreds of thousands of members, all working to ensure total obedience to the Führer*

■ *Below:* SS-Reichsführer Heinrich Himmler (left) presided over a vast SS empire that included the concentration camp network and the Waffen-SS.

■ *Right:* Bitter fighting on the Eastern Front in 1941–43 groomed many Waffen-SS officers for high command in the battle for Normandy. Left to right: Teddy Wisch, Max Wünsche, "Sepp" Dietrich, Fritz Witt.

Hitler was still worried, though. So he decided to expand his élite bodyguard force into the Nazi Party's own mini-army. It would be the only armed force in Germany with an official mandate to take armed action within the borders of the new Third Reich. The German Army would be limited to fighting foreign wars. Thus the Waffen-SS (or armed SS) was born.

It was in these early days that the Waffen-SS developed its unique ethos. Recruits were screened for ethnic purity. They had to be able to trace their "blood line" back through several generations in order to prove they had no Jewish relatives. Any physical imperfections, such as tooth fillings or poor eyesight, also counted against the much sought-after membership of the Waffen-SS.

The prominent public role of the first Waffen-SS unit, the SS *Leibstandarte Adolf Hitler*, guarding their Führer and public buildings in Berlin, quickly led to them being dubbed the "Asphalt Soldiers" by the Wehrmacht (armed forces). They were only fit for parades, the cynics were to claim.

Behind the scenes, Hitler and the head of the overall SS organization, Heinrich Himmler, set in train a number of moves which would turn the Waffen-SS into an élite military formation.

A number of professional staff officers, such as Paul Hausser and Willi Bittrich, were recruited to set up junior officer and non-commissioned officer schools. They would also run staff officer courses and organize logistics. These men ensured professional military discipline and standards endured in

■ *Right:* Paul Hausser was the father of the Waffen-SS panzer divisions. He was considered the equal of many army panzer commanders.

the ranks of the Waffen-SS. Their unit would be a far cry from the political cronyism that was rampant in other parts of Hitler's empire.

The first Waffen-SS units were termed Standarten (roughly equivalent to an army regiment) and they were little more than lightly equipped infantry units. Hitler, however, was determined to ensure his Waffen-SS had the best weapons and equipment. Soon, heavy machine guns, mortars, light artillery and armoured cars were being delivered to Waffen-SS depots.

By the late 1930s the Waffen-SS Standarten had grown into well equipped motorized infantry regiments. They bore names which would later inspire terror, including *Leibstandarte* and *Totenkopf* (Death's Head), and which would be household names during World War II.

As war approached, Hitler decided to regroup. He ordered the Waffen-SS Standarten to be brought together in a single division: the SS-VT. It was included in the war planning for the invasion of Poland, and Hitler hoped it would cover itself in glory in the coming battle against the Poles, whom he considered to be racially sub-human or, in the words of the Nazis, "Untermenschen".

The combat début of the Waffen-SS occurred during the September 1939 invasion of Poland, where the SS-VT Division was assigned to the Wehrmacht's Army Group South. The Poles put up patchy resistance and the SS-VT Division was hardly taxed although, of course, Hitler enthused about his élite unit's performance.

> Hitler was determined to ensure his Waffen-SS had the best weapons and equipment

By the following spring, the Waffen-SS Standarten had been expanded into fully fledged motorized infantry regiments, now boasting assault gun battalions equipped with StuG IIIs. Hitler's favourite *Leibstandarte* Regiment was assigned to support the panzer drive through Holland and Belgium. Here it clashed with Allied forces, and a detachment under the command of Wilhelm Mohnke massacred a squad of captured British troops. The

■ *Below:* "Sepp" Dietrich (front left) and Fritz Witt (front right) observe a training exercise by the *Hitlerjugend* Division in the spring of 1944.

*Totenkopf* Regiment failed to cover itself in glory fighting alongside Erwin Rommel's 7th Panzer Division when it fled after British tanks counterattacked at Arras.

Again Hitler was overjoyed at what he saw as the dazzling combat performance of his Waffen-SS troops, and he ordered yet another expansion. This time there were to be four SS motorized divisions, the *Leibstandarte*, *Das Reich*, *Totenkopf* and *Wiking*. These units were to be the core of the Waffen-SS for the duration of the war, and officers from them would find themselves in great demand as Hitler expanded his élite force into a fully fledged private army of some 35 divisions. It was intended to be an army to rival the Wehrmacht.

The performance of the *Leibstandarte* during the invasion of Yugoslavia and Greece in April 1941 created something of a stir in the army High Command. Its tactical flair and efficiency impressed senior army commanders, who were beginning to appreciate that the Waffen-SS men were not just parade-ground soldiers.

In June 1941 during the invasion of Russia, the four Waffen-SS divisions were in the thick of the action, spearheading the dramatic Blitzkrieg advances deep behind Soviet lines. Hitler's declarations that the war on the Eastern Front was a racial crusade for Lebensraum (or "living space") for the German people was taken up with enthusiasm by the Waffen-SS troops, and they showed themselves more than willing as they executed Soviet prisoners in large numbers, and helped SS *Einsatzgruppen* (Task Forces) murder squads to hunt down and kill Jews.

By the winter, the Soviets had regained their balance and launched a massive counteroffensive. Nazi arrogance meant that Hitler had planned on defeating the Russians by the autumn. Accordingly, there were no supplies of winter clothing for the German troops to wear, or even equipment for them to use. It was only the fanatical resistance of élite units such as the four Waffen-SS divisions which, in the end, held the German front together and prevented a rout. By the spring of 1942, the Waffen-SS units were decimated but, despite their losses, had now managed to firmly establish their fighting reputation.

Hitler's suspicion of his generals was increased after the retreat from Moscow, so he ordered the *Leibstandarte*, *Das Reich* and *Totenkopf* Divisions to be pulled out of Russia and shipped to France. Here they would undergo a thorough programme of rebuilding, and would emerge as the so-called panzergrenadier divisions, although they were to have a full panzer regiment. This extra quota of men was effectively to make them the equivalent of army panzer divisions.

The divisions spent the summer and autumn of 1942 re-equipping and retraining for their new role. This was done under the command of the new SS Panzer Corps of Paul Hausser. The encirclement of the German Sixth Army at Stalingrad in November 1942 forced Hitler to order Hausser's new formation to southern Russia, in order to relieve the 250,000 troops who were trapped in that city. Needless to say, the task was way beyond the capabilities of the Waffen-SS corps and it

■ *Below:* The Waffen-SS pioneered the use of disruptive-pattern camouflage clothing. This is a soldier from the *Totenkopf* Division, a unit that served in the West in 1940 but then spent the rest of the war on the Eastern Front.

ended up being surrounded itself in the Ukrainian city of Kharkov. The SS men were only able to escape thanks to Hausser who, going against the grain, ignored Hitler's orders to fight to the last man.

Hausser and his troops redeemed themselves in the eyes of their Führer by leading the counteroffensive that retook Kharkov in March 1943 and smashing the Soviet forces in the Ukraine. Three months later, Hausser's corps went on to spearhead the German offensive at Kursk and found itself locked in the largest tank battle ever to take place in military history. After over a week of heavy fighting, the Soviet defences held and the Germans were forced on the defensive on the Eastern Front, this time for good. For the next seven months, the *Das Reich*, *Totenkopf* and *Wiking* Divisions fought a series of desperate rearguard actions on the Eastern Front as the Red Army's massive steamroller moved westwards. The

*Leibstandarte* was briefly pulled back to counter the Allied invasion of Italy, but by November 1943 it too was called back to help shore up the Eastern Front. It remained in the East for the next four months, with the result that it suffered horrendous losses while it tried to hold Army Group South's front together.

Buoyed by the success of the Waffen-SS at Kharkov and the failure of the army panzer divisions to relieve Stalingrad, Hitler decided on a major expansion of the Waffen-SS panzer force during the spring of 1943. A second panzer corps headquarters was to be formed, dubbed the I Leibstandarte SS Panzer Corps, under the command of the Führer's old personal favourite, "Sepp" Dietrich. From the outset, it was nominally to contain the *Leibstandarte* Division and a newly formed division, which would be recruited from the ranks of the Nazi youth movement, the

> *Buoyed by the success at Kharkov, Hitler decided on a major expansion of the Waffen-SS panzer force*

■ *Above:* Tiger I heavy tanks in 1943. This was the year they were first used by the Waffen-SS, with the *Leibstandarte*, *Das Reich* and *Totenkopf* Divisions each boasting a company of these powerful tanks.

■ *Above:* By the
spring of 1944, one
panzer battalion in
Waffen-SS panzer
regiments was
equipped with
Panzer IVs.

■ *Left:* By 1944,
the H model Panzer
IV was in wide-
spread use with the
Waffen-SS. It was
fitted with armoured
skirts to provide
protection from
Allied antitank
bazookas.

Hitler Youth or Hitlerjugend. The *Leib-standarte* was to provide a cadre of experienced officers and soldiers for the new corps headquarters and the new division.

By the autumn of 1943 the new units were being formed in training depots in Belgium, although the *Leibstandarte* Division itself would not join them until the following spring, when it was to be released from defensive duties on the Eastern Front.

Not content with this new corps, Hitler wanted more Waffen-SS panzer divisions. Hausser's corps headquarters, now dubbed II SS Panzer Corps, was itself pulled out of Russia after the failed Kursk Offensive and moved to France to begin raising another two Waffen-SS divisions, the *Hohenstaufen* and *Frundsberg*. In the autumn of 1943 a new designation system was introduced, with the panzergrenadier divisions officially being renamed panzer divisions. For example, the premier Waffen-SS unit became the 1st SS Panzer Division *Leibstandarte-SS Adolf Hitler* (or LSSAH).

Although it was not affiliated to the two Waffen-SS panzer corps, the 17th SS Panzergrenadier Division *Götz von Berlichingen* was also formed at this point, and it would later go on to play a prominent part in the battles on the Western Front during the following year.

The new Waffen-SS panzer units were initially slow to take shape, with new recruits and equipment arriving in dribs and drabs. As winter approached and it became clear that the British and Americans would soon launch their invasion of France, the pace of training and equipping took on greater urgency. Soon new tanks, armoured half-tracks and other weapons were flowing to the Waffen-SS in France.

The *Hitlerjugend* Division received the highest priority for men and equipment. Its cadre of *Leibstandarte* instructors were soon whipping the young 17- and 18-year-olds of

■ *Below:* The other tank battalion in Waffen-SS panzer regiments was equipped with Panzer V Panther medium tanks. It proved to be a formidable battlefield weapon.

the division into shape. Lack of time meant the division concentrated on battlefield skills, not parade drills. Tactical exercises with live ammunition were the norm. Panzer crews were sent to tank factories in Germany to help build the vehicles they would soon drive into battle.

The *Hitlerjugend* Division was soon conducting complicated battalion, then regimental, and finally divisional exercises. By the spring of 1944, the division boasted nearly 20,000 soldiers and an almost complete inventory of vehicles and equipment, as well as a high standard of training.

The *Frundsberg* and *Hohenstaufen* Divisions were not quite as lavishly equipped and trained, but nonetheless they were to benefit from a trip to the Eastern Front in April 1944 to help the First Panzer Army break

> *Panzer crews were sent to tank factories to help build the vehicles they would soon drive into battle*

out of a Soviet encirclement. They saw limited action and allowed Hausser's successor, Willi Bittrich, to see his units in battle and to sideline a number of incompetent unit commanders. The troops themselves fought well and showed much potential. They stayed in the Ukraine on temporary "loan" to the Eastern Front until early June, when they were recalled to France to fight in Normandy. On their return they would put up an impressive performance, on a par with the other Waffen-SS units. Bittrich's headquarters team was also first rate, and would later inflict the only strategic defeat on the Allies during the northwest European campaign. This famous defeat was one which would take place at Nijmegen and Arnhem in September 1944.

■ *Below:* The Sturmgeschütz III assault gun combined heavy armour with a powerful 75mm cannon, giving Waffen-SS assault gun battalions a heavy punch.

Languishing in the south of France, the 17th SS Panzergrenadier Division was right at the bottom of the list for receiving new equipment. Its inventory was to number only a single assault gun battalion of StuG IIIs by the time the Allied landings occurred in Normandy in June.

## Rebuilding

Shattered by their experiences on the Eastern Front, the *Leibstandarte* and *Das Reich* Divisions were pulled back to France in the spring of 1944. Here they would be rebuilt in order that they could act as the spearhead for Hitler's counter-invasion strategy. The half-starved and lice-infested remnants of the two divisions were in no shape to do much beyond clean and repair their paltry stocks of weapons and vehicles.

Then the Waffen-SS replacement and supply system started to kick in. The new soldiers and equipment were suddenly beginning to arrive in large quantities. Time was short, however, and the quality of the new recruits left a lot to be desired. Most of them were drafted youngsters, or former Luftwaffe (air force) and navy personnel. They were not of the same ilk as the volunteers who had made their way into the ranks of the élite Waffen-SS divisions earlier in the war. The cadre of *Leibstandarte* and *Das Reich* veterans had to begin almost from scratch. They found themselves teaching these new Waffen-SS men basic soldiering skills while, at the same time, having to indoctrinate them into the special philosophy of their "divisional family".

Crucially, by the late spring of 1944, France and Belgium were hotbeds of resistance sabotage activity, and the Allied air forces had started to concentrate their air attacks on communications links in the run-up to D-Day. This made it almost impossible for the two divisions to take their young recruits out on large-scale manoeuvres. When the invasion came, they would go into battle with half-trained units which were unused to operating together. This would put even greater strain on the remaining Eastern Front veterans.

By the late spring of 1944, the five Waffen-SS panzer and one panzergrenadier division earmarked to repulse the impending

Allied invasion of France boasted some of the most powerful weapons in the German arsenal. The most common tank was the Panzer V Panther. With its sloped armour, wide tracks, and powerful, long 75mm cannon, it could outshoot, outmanoeuvre and out-armour almost every Allied tank.

The Panther could take out the most common Allied tank, the Sherman, at some 2000m (2187yd) range. In marked contrast, a Sherman tank had to close to within 500m

■ *Above:* Members of the *Leibstandarte Adolf Hitler* Division bore their Führer's name on their sleeve cuffs.

(547yd) to stand a chance of penetrating the sloped side armour of the German monster. The lighter Panzer IV was more evenly matched with the Sherman, but as it was equipped with its 75mm gun, would still enjoy a considerable advantage in range. Furthermore, the protection which was given by its add-on armoured skirts was highly efficient in neutralizing both the hollow-charge bazookas and the PIAT guns which would be aimed at them during a concerted Allied attack.

The most feared tank in the German arsenal was called the Tiger I, with its famous 88mm cannon. Its 100mm (3.9in) frontal armour rendered most Allied tank guns useless. The only thing that stood a chance of piercing the frontal armour of the Tiger was the British 17-pounder gun, a weapon which

*The most feared German tank was the Tiger I; its 100mm (3.9in) frontal armour was impenetrable*

boasted a revolutionary discarding tungsten sabot round.

Contrary to popular belief, the monster Tiger II tank never served with the two Waffen-SS heavy panzer battalions in the fighting in Normandy. One army battalion was directed to the Western Front, but it never got to Normandy, as it was caught up in the German rout during August 1944. The Waffen-SS would not see the benefits of these giant tanks until they used them in the Ardennes Offensive of December 1944.

Waffen-SS units also had large numbers of Jagdpanzer IV, StuG III and Marder self-propelled guns at its disposal. These machines were constructed on converted tank chassis, but lacked rotating turrets. Their heavy cannons were mounted low in their hulls, and this had the advantage of

■ *Above:* The Tiger I, with its 88mm cannon and 100mm- (3.9in-) thick frontal armour made it almost invulnerable to Allied armour on the battlefields of Normandy. This tank belongs to the *Das Reich* Division.

■ *Right:* In June 1944 there was only one Waffen-SS Tiger tank unit in France, the 101st SS Heavy Panzer Battalion.

■ *Right:* In the summer of 1944, the antitank firepower of German troops was boosted by the distribution of large numbers of Panzerfaust rockets. This "one shot" weapon was effective up to a range of 100m (110yd).

making them easy to camouflage. They were found to be ideal as defensive weapons. The Jagdpanzer IV was based on a Panzer IV chassis and it had the same long-barrelled 75mm cannon as the Panther and thick, sloped armour.

The StuG III was smaller, being based on the obsolete Panzer III, but it had a useful 75mm cannon. The Marder was a lightly armoured tank hunter, built on a Czech tank chassis, and mounting the incredibly powerful 76.2mm antitank gun, the design of which had been captured from the Russians.

The most powerful antitank units in the Waffen-SS divisions were the 88mm Flak guns of the divisional antiaircraft artillery battalion. These guns could punch through the armour of any Allied tank at an unrivalled range of more than 2500m (2734yd).

At the heart of each Waffen-SS panzer division were two panzergrenadier or mechanized infantry regiments, each of which had an antitank company, supplied either with Marders or towed Pak 40 antitank guns. Panzergrenadier companies were lavishly equipped with the shoulder-fired Panzerschreck antitank rocket launcher, which was copied from the American bazooka, or the "throw-away" one-shot Panzerfaust antitank rocket. These weapons turned every infantry squad into a tank-hunting unit.

One panzergrenadier battalion in each division was mounted in armoured SdKfz 251 halftracks, known as SPWs, to allow it to accompany the panzer battalion into close proximity to the enemy. The other five panzergrenadier battalions were carried in soft-skinned trucks. The divisional reconnaissance battalion also had armoured halftracks, as well as Marders.

Supporting the frontline Waffen-SS troops was an array of powerful artillery systems. A number of self-propelled guns called Wespes, with 105mm guns, and Hummels, with 155mm guns, were mixed with towed 105mm and 150mm guns in divisional artillery regiments.

Each panzergrenadier battalion also had its own infantry gun company which boasted self-propelled 150mm and 75mm guns,

> *The "throw-away" one-shot Panzerfaust antitank rocket turned every infantry squad into a tank-hunting unit*

as well as 120mm heavy mortars. The corps-level firepower was provided by Nebelwerfer multiple rocket launchers.

## Tactics

Their experience of three brutal campaign seasons in Russia had transformed the Waffen-SS panzer divisions into some of the most professional armoured formations the world has ever seen. Under experienced commanders – such as Hausser, Dietrich, Bittrich, Kurt "Panzer" Meyer and Jochen Peiper – the Waffen-SS panzer divisions were trained up and inspired to become masters of their art.

Central to German armoured doctrine was the idea of the all-arms battle group (or Kampfgruppe). Unlike in Allied armies, it was considered routine for the Waffen-SS to quickly form Kampfgruppen. These battle groups would combine tank, panzer-grenadier, antitank, reconnaissance and artillery units and would operate under a single commander. There was no set size or shape of a Kampfgruppe, as these variable factors would depend on the mission and the enemy being faced.

The close-knit Waffen-SS "family" made the formation and functioning of Kampfgruppen even more effective than it was in the Wehrmacht panzer units. These Waffen-SS officers had all served with each other for several years. As a result, they knew exactly how their comrades operated, and could easily become a member of each other's command team. Thus they were able to conduct complex tactical manoeuvres through brief verbal orders which had been issued over the radio net.

Time and time again during the campaigns in the West after D-Day, Waffen-SS Kampfgruppen, despite being rapidly formed, would save the day for the German Army. On the Allied side – in contrast to the Germans' units – the formal and laborious "orders groups" were the norm, making it difficult for their operations to be rapidly improvised.

Mission command (or Auftragstaktik) was at the heart of German Army tactics. Commanders were given an objective to reach and were left to formulate a plan of operation which would achieve the High Command's intent. During both defensive

■ *Below:* The British equivalent of the Panzerfaust was the PIAT gun. Its hollow or shaped-charged warhead punched through the heaviest tank armour with a high-velocity jet of molten metal.

■ *Right:* Heavy mobile firepower for Waffen-SS artillery regiments was provided by the Hummel, a self-propelled 150mm howitzer.

■ *Below:* Waffen-SS corps-level rocket units boasted the Nebelwerfer multiple rocket launcher, which first saw action on the Russian Front (these are captured models being examined by Red Army troops).

and offensive operations, German commanders would decide where exactly the Schwerpunkt (point of main effort) was to be. Once this had been identified, they would concentrate as much of their resources as possible in order to secure it.

In the defensive battles in Normandy, this usually resulted in the Germans trying to hold a key piece of high ground that dominated a large area. Holding the high ground would give an important advantage: devastating artillery as well as tank fire could be brought to bear against the enemy, effecting its retreat.

When the Waffen-SS moved to attack, the same principle was used. However, in their manoeuvres the bulk of the German offensive power would be concentrated against the weakest point in the Allied line. Once success had been achieved, an overwhelming force would be concentrated to reinforce these gains.

The Waffen-SS had learned on the Eastern Front that its tanks were true battle-winning weapons, both in the attack and defence role, as long as they were concentrated and used *en masse*. A division's panzer

battalion would only be committed to action if it could achieve decisive results. It was not to be wasted away in penny packets, holding ground or on limited attacks. The job of holding ground was to be left to the panzergrenadiers, which were to be supported by the antitank units. These two units in turn would often find themselves supported by the Flak battalion's 88mm guns, operating in the direct-fire role.

### Rethinking the battlefield

Once it had been committed to action, a panzer Kampfgruppe would usually boast elements of the SPW battalion, antitank guns and self-propelled artillery. This self-contained force would be able to deal with any likely enemy threat and hold ground once the operation had achieved its objective.

On the whole, the experience the Waffen-SS had gained in Russia was invaluable when it came to fighting the relatively inexperienced British and American divisions which had landed in Normandy. However, no matter how much they had learned, there was one major shortfall: these SS men had never been forced to face massed

> *The Waffen-SS had learned on the Eastern Front that its tanks were battle-winning weapons*

■ *Above:* One battalion of panzergrenadiers in each Waffen-SS panzer division was mounted in SdKfz 251 armoured halftracks.

■ *Right:* Heinrich Himmler had an almost paternal interest in the *Hitlerjugend* Division, which recruited from the ranks of the Nazi Youth movement and bore the Führer's name. He is seen here inspecting some of its young soldiers in France in the spring of 1944.

Allied airpower. The paralyzing effect of the overhead presence of British Typhoons or American Mustangs was to force a rethink by the Waffen-SS commanders. They realized that they would have to change the way they moved their troops around the battlefield. It soon became apparent that the massed tank attacks which had worked so well for them on the Eastern Front were, once executed in the West, extremely vulnerable to devastating Allied air attack.

> One thing the Waffen-SS never lacked in abundance throughout the war was fighting spirit

### Fighting spirit

One thing the Waffen-SS – particularly its officer corps – never lacked in abundance throughout the duration of the war was fighting spirit. A major factor in nurturing and maintaining the fighting spirit of the Waffen-SS panzer divisions was their strong sense of unit identity. Both officers and non-commissioned officers alike served almost exclusively in the same regiment or divisions throughout their time in uniform. They had come to know and trust their comrades in arms, and had shared successes and hardships. Each division also had its own distinct set of characteristics.

The *Leibstandarte* was the élite of the élite. It was the first unit to be formed and the Führer took a personal interest in the division which bore his name, receiving priority for recruits and equipment.

*Das Reich* had been hardened by years on the Eastern Front, but by 1944 was an unhappy unit under a martinet commander, Heinz Lammerding. The *Hitlerjugend* adopted many of the traditions of the Nazi Youth movement and was not strong on military formalities. Many of its officers were former *Leibstandarte* men who were determined to prove themselves as good as their old comrades.

The *Hohenstaufen* and *Frundsberg* Divisions were new units but, despite this, were very professional in the way they conducted themselves. In 1944, soldiers of the Waffen-SS panzer divisions all believed that they were serving in the best units in the world. Every single soldier considered himself to be utterly invincible.

The leadership of the Waffen-SS panzer force had developed and matured during the course of the war. There were a number of distinct groups within the Waffen-SS and they all – to varying degrees – meshed together to produce very effective fighting units. There was a rump of senior officers who were all hardcore Nazis, such as "Sepp" Dietrich, who had loyally served Hitler for two decades.

Senior officers such as "Sepp" Dietrich were the owners of the power, positions and lavish property under Hitler's regime. Moreover, they were passionate believers in Hitler's cause, particularly his racial war against the Jewish and Slav "Untermenschen" in the East. Men like Dietrich never had any pretensions to be military geniuses, and relied on professional soldiers like Hausser, Bittrich and Fritz Kraemer to run things for them. Dietrich was later to enjoy promotion to the rank of SS-Oberstgruppenführer, or the equivalent of an army lieutenant-general, which many considered to be a serious case of over-promotion. However, what mattered most to Hitler was Dietrich's loyalty, not his tactical skill. Over the years, Dietrich did manage to pick up the basics of tank tactics; indeed, he had served in the first German tank unit during World War I. He was also far from stupid and would listen to advice from subordinates. His specialty was motivating men to fight and die for the Führer. However, after four years of war, he was now beginning to show the first signs of being disillusioned with the hopeless struggle. Despite this disenchantment, Dietrich's loyalty to his old boss kept him fighting.

Hausser and Bittrich were the military intellectuals of the Waffen-SS. They were to provide it with its military professionalism and, as a result, they were well respected by their army colleagues. Hitler, however, never quite trusted them. He once called Hausser "crafty fox" in a very uncomplimentary way. However, they were practical, down-to-earth soldiers, and by 1944 they were no longer

■ *Below:* Supplementing the heavy Hummel was the 105mm Wespe self-propelled gun.

■ *Above:* The "brains" of "Sepp" Dietrich for much of the war was his loyal chief of staff, Fritz Kraemer, seen here with map at I SS Panzer Corps' headquarters in Normandy. Note the Knight's Cross at his neck.

convinced that Germany would be able to win the war. There was a small core of Himmler cronies in the Waffen-SS panzer divisions. They found their way into senior command posts through Himmler's personal patronage, and because of this nepotism, they were considered "untouchable", even if they proved to be totally incompetent. Lammerding of *Das Reich* and the *Hitlerjugend* Division's Mohnke were examples of the individuals who would fit into this category.

## The leaders of men

Almost all Waffen-SS combat regiments and battalions in France in 1944 were commanded by hardcore veterans. These were men who had worked their way up through the ranks of their divisions. Most of them had started out their military life as junior officers in the opening days of the war and, by a process of natural selection, ended up shouldering much of the responsibility for the fight against the Allies. The likes of

Meyer, Peiper, Fritz Witt, Max Wünsche, Teddy Wisch and tank ace Michael Wittmann were all in their late twenties or early thirties, and could only be described as "natural leaders of men".

These highly skilled soldiers were men who led from the front. As a result of their actions, they took great pride in accumulating injuries and medals at an alarming rate. They were expert practitioners of armoured warfare. Often their presence on the battlefield was enough to a turn around a calamitous situation and restore the troops' morale.

Unlike British and American officers – who did not wear their medals on the battlefield – Waffen-SS officers made a great show of their decorations. This was particularly the case if they had won the famous Knight's Cross for bravery in battle (worn at the neck). Some of them even wore them with their camouflage combat smocks. They were totems of their own bravery in past battles, and their appearance also served to make their followers aspire to win these medals.

These young Waffen-SS officers were totally ruthless, yet at the same time their troops idolized them. This was largely because of their willingness to lead from the front. It was as if they hoped that the aura of invincibility that surrounded them would rub off on the men whom they led.

Unlike some of the older Waffen-SS hands, they had far from given up the fight, and now that the opportunity to achieve fame and notoriety had arisen, they were hungry for glory. Their wishes would soon come true.

## Locked into war

For the rank-and-file men serving in the Waffen-SS, their enthusiastic willingness to fight was due to a combination of various factors. Since Hitler's accession to power, the population of Germany had been subject to daily bombardments of Nazi propaganda. These sinister messages were cleverly crafted so that they whipped up support for Hitler's warped ideology. The school and university systems were fertile recruiting ground for the Nazi Party, and the indoctrination of those youngsters was a major objective for Hitler's henchmen. The outbreak of war accelerated this process of indoctrination. Once the Allied bombers started raiding major

German cities in massive numbers from late 1942 onwards, the German people could see for themselves what little pity they would evoke from such a ruthless enemy. In the aftermath and carnage of the mass bombings, it was easy for Hitler's propaganda genius, Josef Goebbels, to declare total war and for German civilians to be swept along by his enthusiasm for the conflict.

With Berlin and other cities being systematically turned into ruins by Allied bombers, German soldiers knew they were locked into a fight to the finish. The men who had served on the Eastern Front also realized that Germany would face no mercy if the Soviets ever broke through and were allowed to push into the Reich.

Even though by 1944 the Waffen-SS found itself relying increasingly on conscripted manpower – including former Luftwaffe and navy personnel – it would nevertheless contain a higher proportion of volunteers than were to be found in line army units. These were a mix of hard core Nazis, professional soldiers seeking rapid career advancement, and a sprinkling of adventurers who wanted to taste the excitement and horror of battle. Their wishes would soon be granted in the killing fields of Normandy.

■ *Below:* Nazi propaganda chief Josef Goebbels (centre) had convinced the German people that they could still win the war, if the Allies were driven back into the sea after any invasion of France.

# CHAPTER 3

# INVASION FRONT

## German plans for the defeat of the Allied invasion of France.

I n the spring of 1944, at depots and training camps all over Belgium and France, veteran Waffen-SS instructors were hard at work trying to knock thousands of new recruits into shape to meet the coming Allied invasion of northwest Europe.

Due to the lamentable state of German intelligence, Field Marshal Erwin Rommel, the commander of Army Group B, had no firm intelligence about where the Allied troops would come ashore. Aerial photographs showed huge camps in southern England packed with tanks, artillery and supplies, while ports around the British coast were chock-a-block with ships and landing craft. All that was certain was that this immense force would attempt to open the long-awaited second front in a matter of months.

### The Atlantic Wall

For the famous "Desert Fox", time was of the essence. When he toured France on an inspection of the Atlantic Wall coastal defences during December 1943, Rommel was far from impressed. France had long been a backwater of the war. It was where German units would be sent to recuperate after suffering a mauling in Russia. After being appointed commander of the invasion coast, which stretched from the French border to northern Holland, Rommel had been trying to knock the last vestiges of complacency out of his rag-tag collection of just under 60 divisions. He ordered a major effort to reinforce the beach defences with minefields and fortifications. Millions of tons of concrete were poured into the ground to build

■ **Left:** Despite the millions of tons of concrete and heavy batteries like this one, the Atlantic Wall was breached in 1944.

■ *Right:* Field Marshal Gerd von Rundstedt (centre) believed the panzer reserves should be held back from the coast for a massed counterattack.

bunkers and gun positions overlooking every possible landing site on the French coast. Inland, Rommel wanted strong armoured forces close at hand to defeat any Allied troops that did manage to get ashore.

The Waffen-SS provided the bulk of Rommel's armoured reserve, comprising six of the 11 panzer and panzergrenadier divisions available to the Western Front. Except for a brief period in Italy when he worked with the *Leibstandarte* Division, Rommel had never commanded Waffen-SS divisions, but he quickly formed a favourable impression of them and their commanders. Touring their training grounds, Rommel could see their superb equipment and rigorous training schedules quickly bearing fruit. That was more than could be said for a number of army divisions. Rommel was shocked at the state of the infantry divisions manning the invasion defences along the coast, which were staffed mainly by former Russian and Polish prisoners. Their fighting potential was minimal. Some of the army panzer divisions were not much better, with the famous 21st

Panzer Division having to make do with captured French tanks and trucks in many of its battalions. Such problems only increased Rommel's reliance on the Waffen-SS, which had first call on replacement manpower, new weapons and equipment.

## Armoured fist

Rommel threw himself into his mission with a vengeance, setting a punishing schedule of inspection visits around France and trips to the Führer's headquarters in East Prussia to secure more men and resources for his command. He spent hours locked in fruitless meetings with Hitler to secure backing for his counter-invasion strategy.

From his experience in North Africa and Italy, Rommel believed that the Allies had to be defeated on the landing beaches, otherwise they would be able to consolidate a bridgehead and bring their overwhelming superiority in materiel to bear against the thinly stretched German defenders. Rommel believed he would have little chance in a war of attrition in France. Any invasion would

■ *Above:* Rommel, seen here inspecting beach defences, wanted the panzers positioned close to the beaches to stop the Allies establishing a bridgehead on the first day of any invasion.

■ *Right:* Hitler refused to make up his mind about which anti-invasion strategy to follow.

have to be smashed within 24 hours, so the panzer divisions should be based close to the coast, ready to strike.

Rommel's immediate superior in France, the 71-year-old Gerd von Rundstedt, disagreed, and argued that it would be better to mass all the panzer reserves inland as a huge strike force, and then launch one knock-out blow against the Allied bridgehead. Luftwaffe bombers and Admiral Karl Dönitz's U-boat fleet would also be able to cut the Allies' supply lines, leaving them isolated in France.

Furious arguments raged between Rommel and his commander-in-chief. Allied airpower would slaughter the panzers columns as they marched to the coast, said Rommel. The "Desert Fox" had little confidence in German air and seapower being able to influence the coming battle. SS-Oberstgruppenführer Paul Hausser and SS-Obergruppenführer Josef "Sepp" Dietrich, the commanders of the two SS panzer corps, also weighed in to the argument on the side of Rundstedt. Their experience in Russia told them that a mass attack would have more chance of success. Rommel countered that they had never had to fight under conditions of Allied air supremacy.

The lack of intelligence on Allied intentions also complicated Rommel's planning. While most German commanders in France

■ *Right:* Rommel and "Sepp" Dietrich (right) worked well together to build up the panzer reserves in France during the spring of 1944.

were convinced that the Allies would strike across the Straits of Dover to seize the Pas de Calais, the possibility of an invasion farther west in Normandy could not be excluded.

With his generals unable to agree on a common strategy, Hitler not surprisingly was able to force his own strategy on the invasion-front commanders. Even though his astrologer told him to expect an invasion in Normandy, Hitler decreed that the bulk of the German forces in the West would be based within striking distance of the Pas de Calais. This included the two SS panzer corps, until II SS Panzer Corps was temporarily dispatched to the Eastern Front in April 1944. He backed Rundstedt's idea of a concentrated counterattack.

In April 1944, Hitler took on board some of Rommel's ideas and decided to move some panzer units westwards to cover the Normandy beaches. The *Hitlerjugend* Division was shipped to new bases northwest of Paris, within a day's drive of Normandy, and Dietrich soon followed with his corps headquarters. The *Leibstandarte* was still refitting and remained behind in Belgium. Dietrich's force of one division and corps heavy tank battalions was poised with three army panzer divisions to strike at any landing in Normandy. Hitler gave Rundstedt and Rommel the authority to move the three army divisions, but the Führer had to give his approval for any other panzer units, including the Waffen-SS, to move towards any invasion beach. This was a classic Hitler muddle. It meant Rommel would have insufficient forces to kill off any Allied bridgehead at birth, while Rundstedt was unable to muster his 11 panzer division force to strike at the Allies *en masse*. This convoluted command arrangement would bedevil the German response when the invasion did occur in June 1944.

## Fight to the finish

These arguments were far from the minds of the Waffen-SS tank crews and panzergrenadiers training in France and Belgium in the spring of 1944. They were focused on the coming battle with the British and Americans. Day after day, their commanders stressed that the outcome of the war would turn on the coming battle. If the Allies could be quickly thrown back into the sea, then Germany would have won a key breathing space to turn its attention eastwards once again and drive back the Soviets, who were already on Poland's eastern border.

For the Waffen-SS, their Führer's struggle against the Soviets was a crusade for racial survival. The threat from the Western Allies was a diversion from this battle that had to be quickly resolved, to release them to once again take on the Russians. On his inspections, Rommel told the Waffen-SS men that the Allies would not be able to recover from the defeat of their invasion. If the Allies failed to secure a bridgehead in Europe, it could take years for them to regain their strength to make another attempt (which was correct), perhaps forcing them to sue for peace, or so said Hitler.

This strategic assessment was one of Hitler's more accurate. It was shared by the Supreme Allied Commander, US Army General Dwight D. Eisenhower. He also took the view that the fate of the war would turn on the success or failure of the invasion. The Waffen-SS would soon have to face its most important battle.

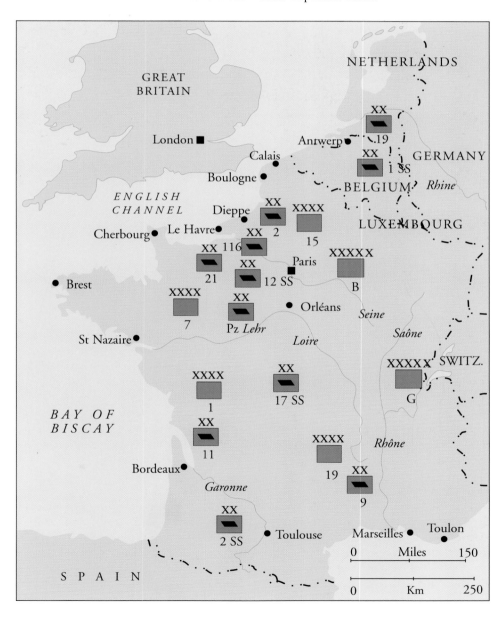

■ *Left:*
**The disposition of German Army groups, armies and panzer divisions on D-Day, 6 June 1944.**

# CHAPTER 4

# CARNAGE AT CAEN

## The 12th SS Panzer Division and the defence of Caen.

In its billets northwest of Paris, the men of the *Hitlerjugend* Division could clearly hear the waves of Allied bombers passing overhead on the morning of 6 June 1944. This performance was heavier than usual. Throughout the early hours of the morning, a steady stream of phone calls alerted the division to the fact that parachute landings were taking place all over Normandy. The divisional commander, 36-year-old SS-Brigadeführer Fritz Witt, put his command on alert. Commanders frantically roused their troops from bed, and reconnaissance parties were formed, ready for any move to counter the invasion.

In the German High Command, confusion reigned. No one was sure where the Allies had landed or in what strength. Rommel, Rundstedt and Hitler all prevaricated, fearing the landing in Normandy was just a feint to distract attention from an assault in the Pas de Calais, or in the mouth of the Somme. A reconnaissance force was sent to the coast south of the Somme at 02:30 hours but the rest of the *Hitlerjugend* Division had to wait for orders. Reports were coming in every couple of minutes, but there was still no concrete information on the Allied attack.

At 05:00 hours orders were issued for the division to begin concentrating at Lisieux in eastern Normandy. It took several hours for the troops to get on the road, and they spent the rest of the day moving westwards under relentless Allied air attack. Swarms of fighter-bombers – "Jagdbombers" or "Jabos" as they were known to the German panzer crews – were scouting ahead of the Allied bridgehead

■ *Left:* A smashed Panzer IV in Caen, which was turned into a bloody battleground strewn with rubble and wrecked tanks.

■ *Above:* An award ceremony for *Hitlerjugend* Division members involved in the fighting around Caen.

twisted and smoking wreckage. Refugee columns clogged the roads, and this was responsible for further hindering the movement of German troops towards Normandy. As a result of these obstacles, it would be nightfall before the division found itself anywhere near striking distance of the Allied bridgehead.

## The Allies have landed

The German High Command was still locked in confusion about what to do with the panzer reserves. By mid-afternoon on 6 June it was clear that the Normandy landing was in fact no feint. Although the Germans did not have precise information, Allied records showed that 55,000 men were firmly established ashore in five main bridgeheads. Only in the late afternoon were the first orders for counterattacks issued to the panzer reserves. The 21st Panzer Division was already in

on the lookout for German columns. Some 20 vehicles were destroyed and more than 80 *Hitlerjugend* soldiers killed or wounded in the attacks. More important than the materiel and human losses was the delay caused as the Waffen-SS columns had to stop, take cover and weave their way past

■ *Left:* To reach the battlefield around Caen, *Hitlerjugend* Division troops spent almost two days on the road from their assembly areas.

■ *Right:* Allied fighter-bombers harassed the *Hitlerjugend* columns as they moved towards the Normandy battle front.

■ *Above:* The *Hitlerjugend's* Panzer IVs arrived west of Caen on the morning of 7 June to spearhead the division's counterattack.

action north of Caen against the British bridgeheads. Accordingly, the *Hitlerjugend* and *Panzer Lehr* Divisions were ordered to move against the British beaches. They were under the command of "Sepp" Dietrich's I SS Panzer Corps.

The *Leibstandarte* Division remained in Belgium to counter the threat of an Allied landing in the Pas de Calais, the region which so dogged Hitler. In the meantime, the *Das Reich* and the 17th SS Panzergrenadier Divisions began moving northwards from southwest France. Despite their determination, it would be at least a week before they managed to reach the invasion front. It would also be six days until Hitler finally agreed to release II SS Panzer Corps from the Eastern Front in order that it might return to

Normandy. Far from being able to hammer the Allies with a decisive, knock-out blow, the Germans ended up committing their reserves piecemeal in a desperate bid to shore up a crumbling front.

While Dietrich was easily able to establish contact with his old comrade, Witt, he nevertheless had great problems in trying to link up with the 21st Panzer Division or the remnants of the infantry divisions resisting the British north of the large Norman city of Caen.

*The Germans committed their reserves piecemeal in a desperate bid to shore up a crumbling front*

Dietrich and other staff officers from the Waffen-SS criss-crossed the German front in order to try to pull together some sort of cohesion. All during the night they worked out various formulae for counterattack plan after counterattack plan. But all of their of their plans were rapidly overtaken by events. The commander of the 21st Panzer Division could not be found at his command post, and this was to further frustrate plans to mount a joint attack with the *Hitlerjugend* Division.

Of even more concern was the fact that the arrival of the *Hitlerjugend* Division was still stalled because of the chaotic conditions on the roads. The *Panzer Lehr* Division was even further behind, and would not arrive at the front for days. In the meantime, thousands more Allied troops and tanks were rapidly pouring ashore.

The planned mass panzer attack for the following day had to be scrapped. The most that could be expected was for the *Hitlerjugend* Division to go in, with support from 21st Panzer. The first Kampfgruppe of the *Hitlerjugend* Division to reach the front was based on the 25th SS Panzergrenadier Regiment, commanded by the famous SS-Standartenführer Kurt "Panzer" Meyer.

## Kurt "Panzer" Meyer

Only 34 years old, Meyer was an aggressive and determined officer who would claim fame for being the youngest German divisional commander of World War II. He would also later be accused of being the perpetrator of war crimes because of the merciless killing of Canadian prisoners of war during the coming battle.

Supreme self-confidence – which, some said, bordered on arrogance – was Meyer's trademark, and when he arrived at the 21st Panzer's headquarters during the early hours of 7 June in order to coordinate the coming

■ *Below:* A *Hitlerjugend* Panzer IV rumbles through Caen. Note the armoured "skirt' to defeat Allied antitank rockets.

attack, he did not win any friends. He took one look at the situation map and left the army officers in no doubt as to how totally unimpressed he was by their assessment of the threat posed by the Allied forces in the Normandy bridgehead.

"Little fish! We'll throw them back into the sea in the morning." For all his bravado, they could be absolutely sure that Meyer was not joking, either.

Meyer was to push forward on the left flank of the 21st Panzer, after forming up on the western edge of Caen itself. His objective was simple: to reach the coast. By first light, only a few companies of the 25th Regiment were in place on the start-line, with the remainder still moving around the southern suburbs of Caen. In the meantime, the petrol shortages and traffic chaos meant that the 26th SS Panzergrenadier Regiment and the *Hitlerjugend*'s Panther tank battalion would not be in position to attack at the earliest until the following day.

This was to be a worrying time for Meyer as he surveyed the battle front from his command post in the Ardennes abbey, 4.8km (3 miles) outside Caen. At 10:00 hours, his Panzer IV battalion with 50 tanks finally arrived, followed by more of his Waffen-SS panzergrenadiers.

The attack was fixed for 16:00 hours, with two panzergrenadier units advancing line abreast. They were to be supported in

■ *Left:* The *Hitlerjugend*'s first battles in Normandy were run by, left to right, Kurt "Panzer" Meyer, Fritz Witt and Max Wünsche.

■ *Right:* Hundreds of Canadian Shermans were thrown into action against the meagre defence lines of the *Hitlerjugend* Division.

their efforts by large numbers of heavy tanks and artillery.

During the early afternoon, Meyer watched from the Abbey's high tower as the Canadian 3rd Division – which was known to contain three full infantry brigades and was backed by hundreds of tanks – started to form up for a major attack. Blissfully unaware that the *Hitlerjugend* Division was in its path, the Canadian 9th Brigade and a regiment of tanks began their advance. To observers, they looked as unthreatening as a unit which was on a training exercise during peacetime.

Making a split-second decision, Meyer junked his deliberate attack plan and instead decided to lay a devastating ambush for the Allied force. By now this force had bypassed one of his advance panzergrenadier units and was heading deep into the German rear with Carpiquet airfield as its objective. All of Meyer's 88mm-armed tanks and antitank guns which were in hull-down positions on a ridge near the abbey were ordered to hold their fire until the Canadian 9th Brigade and the tanks drove into the centre of Meyer's killing zone. The Panzer IV companies were ordered to move quickly along the hedge-lined roads before taking up vantage fire positions on the flanks of the Canadian line of advance.

### Panzer power strikes

Meyer waited until the Canadians were within 200m (219yd) of his lines before giving the order "Achtung panzer – marsche!" Panzer crews powered up their engines and moved into position.

Fire started raining down on the Canadian brigade. Stuart and Sherman tanks began to explode after taking devastating hits from the *Hitlerjugend* panzers. Then Meyer's I Battalion of panzergrenadiers was launched into the shell-shocked remains of the Canadian 9th Brigade.

The battle lasted for six hours as the two forces became intermingled. Company sized groups of Canadians were surrounded by Meyer's troops in the small Normandy villages. Many fought to the last man, while others surrendered when they ran out of ammunition. Heavy Canadian artillery caused many German casualties that had to be evacuated on the backs of Panzer IVs. A Canadian counterattack now regained some of the lost ground, so Meyer ordered his two remaining panzergrenadier battalions into action. II Battalion with three companies of Panzer IVs led the way in a tight wedge formation. This restored the situation and the Canadians were soon in retreat.

The panzer battalion command group now stumbled into a troop of Shermans and were killed. I Battalion, with one Panzer IV company, pushed forward into a sector held by British troops of the Royal Ulster Rifles. The two forces soon became intermingled in the village of Cambes. British Sherman tanks shot up German gun positions before being knocked out by Panzerfaust teams, while Panzer IVs suffered heavy losses from Allied antitank guns. Both sides now pulled back to defensive positions on either side of Cambes.

Meyer was all set to push forward when he spotted another Canadian brigade moving south around his right flank. The 21st

> *Stuart and Sherman tanks started to explode after taking devastating hits from Hitlerjugend panzers*

Panzer Division's attack had still not started and Meyer was afraid his flank would be turned. His Kampfgruppe was just not strong enough to take on all of the 3rd Canadian Division, so he reluctantly called a halt to his attack. As night fell, the 25th Regiment adopted defensive positions and easily saw off a series of night probes by the Canadians.

Two Canadian regiments – the North Nova Scotia Highlanders and Sherbrooke Fusiliers – lost more than 500 men killed, wounded or captured, as well as 28 tanks destroyed or damaged, during the day's engagement. Meyer lost some 300 casualties and 9 tanks. At the time, many of Meyer's troops were despondent, as they had failed to reach their objective. Given the odds, however, they had achieved an amazing result, stopping the Canadian advance in its tracks and thereby thwarting General Sir Bernard Montgomery's plans to seize Caen on that same day.

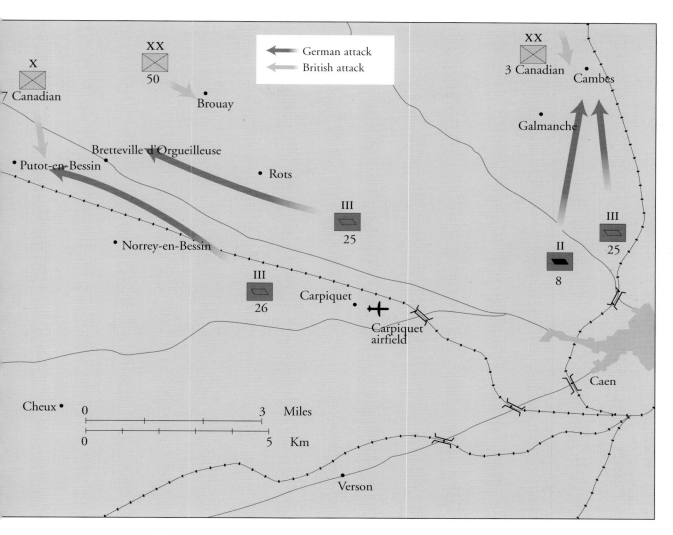

X
7 Canadian

XX
50
• Brouay

German attack
British attack

XX
3 Canadian
• Cambes

• Galmanche

Bretteville d'Orgueilleuse
• Rots

• Putot-en-Bessin

III
25

III
25

II
8

• Norrey-en-Bessin

III
26

Carpiquet

Carpiquet
airfield

Caen

Cheux •
0 _____ 3 Miles

0 _____ 5 Km

Verson

■ *Above:* The
*Hitlerjugend*
**successfully**
**defeated a number**
**of Allied attacks to**
**the north and**
**northwest of Caen**
**in early June 1944.**

The following day saw Meyer forced to consolidate his small force until the rest of the division was in a position to attack. Out on the left flank, the *Hitlerjugend*'s reconnaissance battalion tried to link up with any German units still putting up resistance, but Meyer's flank was effectively hanging in open air. The halftrack-mounted reconnaissance troops had a lively day, skirmishing with British troops and tanks of the Durham Light Infantry and 4th/7th Dragoon Guards, convincing them that the German front was far stronger than it really was.

Pushing westwards from Caen, small *Hitlerjugend* patrols in SdKfz 250 half-tracks or SdKfz 234 eight-wheeled armoured cars were trying to find out the extent of the Allied advance southwards. Operating in small groups, the German vehicles soon

started engaging Allied advance patrols. By the evening, the battalion was pulled back to form a firm defensive line to cover the deployment of the 26th Panzergrenadier Regiment.

On 8 June, SS-Oberstürmbannführer Wilhelm Mohnke's 26th Regiment was to attack at first light. This was Mohnke's return to combat duty after almost three years recovering from the loss of a foot in Yugoslavia and serving in a number of administrative jobs. His comrades were watching closely to see if he held up under the pressure. The division's Panther tank battalion was still delayed by fuel shortages, so his three panzergrenadier battalions would go into the attack with no tank support.

Mohnke's task was to drive back the Allied units which had been detected by the

■ *Above:* British
infantry soon joined
the battle against
the *Hitlerjugend*,
alongside the
Canadian 3rd
Infantry Division.
This is a machine
gunner from the
Durham Light
Infantry.

reconnaissance battalion as they moved forward on the extreme left of the *Hitlerjugend* Division's flank. Mohnke's men proceeded forward on foot, supported only by SdKfz 251/22 armoured halftracks armed with 75mm guns.

First into action at dawn was the 26th Regiment's I Battalion. Its men were tasked with seizing the village of Norrey-en-Bessin. Without armour support, the attack soon found itself bogged down. When the lead panzergrenadier companies were caught in the open by Canadian machine-gun, mortar and artillery fire, the Germans had to admit

defeat. After many of the company and platoon commanders had been killed or wounded, the Waffen-SS attack was eventually repulsed.

In the centre of the regiment's attack was the II Battalion, which had been assigned the village of Putot-en-Bessin as its objective. Due to strong artillery support, the II Battalion was able to reach the village and surround three companies of the Canadian Royal Winnipeg Rifles inside a few buildings. The Canadians tried to escape, but the Waffen-SS killed or captured most of them. The British 24th Lancers counterattacked in response to the success of the Germans, getting in amongst the panzergrenadiers. More than 40 Germans were captured in this foray before the III Battalion's self-propelled anti-tank company intervened with its Marders and drove the British off.

As dusk was falling, the 7th Canadian Brigade launched a major counterattack, with heavy artillery and tank support. Under massive pressure, the II Battalion pulled out of Putot-en-Bessin, losing some 100 men in the action.

Meanwhile Mohnke's armoured personnel carrier-mounted panzergrenadier unit, III Battalion, went into attack on the extreme left flank of his regiment. It rapidly relieved a badly shot-up panzergrenadier battalion of the *Panzer Lehr* Division in Brouay and then spent the day fending off one attack after the other from British tanks.

### Outgunned by the British

Out on the *Hitlerjugend*'s extreme left flank, the reconnaissance battalion found itself outgunned by the British 8th Armoured Brigade. Pin-pointed by British scouts, the battalion was now targeted by three artillery regiments and two battleships. The battalion's command post was wiped out in a single salvo, and its companies were also targeted, with total losses running to 80 men.

As the evening began, it was Meyer's 25th Regiment's turn to go forward on the attack. The offensive would enjoy the support of the *Hitlerjugend*'s Panther tank battalion. In a daring night attack, Meyer punched through the Canadian lines and surrounded a regimental headquarters based inside the village of Bretteville d'Orgueilleuse. This attack, which was westward from his position, was intended to strike at the exposed flank of the Canadian brigade which was counterattacking Mohnke's regiment.

The 25th Regiment's reconnaissance company followed up on its motorcycles, close behind the two companies of tanks, and they were to storm Canadian trenches after the panzer assault. Panzergrenadiers were then to mop up the Canadian position. In characteristic fashion, Meyer went into

> *In characteristic fashion, Meyer went into battle on a motorcycle side car, his way of motivating his men*

■ *Left:* The fighting outside Caen was intense, with heavy casualties on both sides. This soldier from the Durham Light Infantry has been lucky.

battle riding on a motorcycle side car, his way of motivating his men to give their all, but showing how impetuous the 32-year-old leader could be in the heat of battle.

As they approached the village, the Panthers fanned out into attack formation and gathered speed. A wall of antitank gunfire hit them as they got to within 200m (219yd) of the village, knocking out several tanks. Spurred on by Meyer's presence, the tanks started to blast apart the village, with burning tanks and buildings turning night into day. The Canadians fired their salvos of parachute flares above the German tanks, silhouetting them, thereby providing excellent targets as well as temporarily blinding the Panther crews. Meyer now changed his tactics, sending groups of tanks and panzergrenadiers to penetrate the village from the north and south, thus avoiding the heavy antitank gunfire.

The Canadians retreated into a series of fortified strongpoints to try to hold off the attack. Meyer's Panthers were able to get into the village, where they proceeded to shoot up Canadian bunkers and trucks.

In a crazy night battle, some 22 Panthers circled the Canadian command post of the Regina Rifles Regiment, with Meyer darting in between them in his motorcycle! The I Battalion had not been able to penetrate the Canadian defences, leaving the Panthers largely unsupported. In the end Canadian PIAT bazookas and antitank guns firing new sabot rounds knocked out six of the Panthers, so Meyer reluctantly called off the attack as dawn was breaking.

Small groups of German motorcyclists had managed to get into the village, and were eventually able to make their escape back to German lines. Meyer's foray had been an expensive exercise, and had left 155 men dead, wounded or prisoners. The commander of the *Hitlerjugend*'s panzer regiment, Max Wünsche, had gone along for the ride on a borrowed tank, but for all his bravado, had not been as lucky as Meyer and had ended up wounded.

> *Canadian infantry joined in, machine-gunning the survivors as they made their escape on foot*

■ *Right:* Canadian infantry and tank reserves were thrown into the battle in an attempt to overwhelm the *Hitlerjugend* defenders of Caen.

■ *Above:* Allied tank and infantry cooperation left much to be desired, and hampered attempts to open a gap in the *Hitlerjugend*'s lines.

Allied pressure on Mohnke's Regiment continued during 9 June, with a series of attacks by both British and Canadian troops. The 8th Armoured Brigade continued to probe into the *Hitlerjugend*'s reconnaissance battalion, which now had been joined by a Panther company, attached to beef-up its firepower. They traded fire with British Shermans all day, but were not able to hold back their advance. Only the arrival of elements of the *Panzer Lehr* Division could neutralize this threat to *Hitlerjugend*'s flank.

Meyer tried again with another raid by the Panther battalion which took place early on in the afternoon, but lost seven tanks to Canadian antitank fire. He sent a company of 12 tanks forward without infantry and artillery, expecting the surprise and shock effect to unnerve the defenders who were now dug-in in the village of Norrey-en-Bessin. The tanks formed a long line and headed out across open fields towards their objective when, one by one, the Panthers started to fall victim to Canadian tanks in ambush positions. Each Panther caught fire,

and all the crew who escaped were badly burned. Canadian infantry then joined in, machine-gunning the survivors as they made their escape on foot. The whole episode was a dismal failure, with 15 men dead and 20 badly wounded.

The failure of the attack was a major problem for the *Hitlerjugend* Division, because it left a Canadian strongpoint jutting southwards into the line between the 25th and 26th Regiments. During the early hours of 10 June, the division's pioneer battalion was to go into action to neutralize the position. German pioneers were considered élite infantry, specializing in assault operations and, as a result, great gains were expected to be made from their attack.

Under cover of darkness, the pioneers tried to approach the Canadian position in silence, but they were soon detected. Heavy mortar and artillery fire began raining down on the exposed pioneers. They managed to reach the edge of the village before the attack stalled. For most of the following day the men were pinned down, finding themselves

■ *Above:* The USS *Nevada* and other Allied battleships made life very uncomfortable for the German defenders in Normandy, raining down a constant stream of high explosives far inland.

unable either to advance or to retreat. By late afternoon, the pioneers managed to pull back, but they were forced to leave 80 dead or wounded behind. Allied naval gunfire support continued to pound the *Hitlerjugend* Division, and it was to have a devastating effect as 14in and 16in shells rained down on Caen. The use of altitude fuses meant the Allied shelling resulted in hot shrapnel raining down on German positions. When not actually fighting, Meyer had his men digging bunkers, trenches, artillery gun pits and panzer shelters. By digging large scrapes to drive their tanks into, the panzer crews protected their vehicles from the unrelenting barrages which

■ *Right:* With German defences solidifying, the Allies had quickly to rethink their strategy and tactics at Caen.

■ *Right:* British
General Bernard
Montgomery
(standing in car)
visits the Normandy
bridgehead in early
June to work out his
next move.

smashed radio antenna, destroyed sighting optics or, in some extreme cases, ripped off tank turrets.

## Firepower mismatch

Time and time again, Dietrich tried to muster his panzer divisions for a corps-level counterattack, but he was constantly having to reorganize his forces to plug holes in the front. The *Panzer Lehr* Division had still not arrived in strength, leaving the *Hitlerjugend* Division to hold the line to the west of Caen for another day. It was reinforced by the arrival of I SS Panzer Corps' artillery regiment, but this boost did little to even out the mismatch between German and Allied firepower on the Normandy Front.

*Shermans were stalked by German Panzerfaust teams through village streets and country lanes*

The Canadians were now joined by the British 50th Division for a major attack on the afternoon of 11 June. The reconnaissance battalion again proved its worth as a hard-hitting mobile strike force. A company of *Hitlerjugend* Panthers and the division's reconnaissance battalion raced to block their line of advance. Holding their fire until the British tanks had raced ahead of their infantry, machine gunners in the reconnaissance halftracks then raked the ranks of the

Green Howards Regiment. Lying in ambush, the Panthers picked off the British Shermans of the 4th/7th Dragoon Guards from a hill-top firing line. The British attack faltered when one Sherman that had penetrated to with a few yards of the German battalion's command post was knocked out by a 75mm antitank gun. The arrival of the reserve Panther company sent the British reeling backwards. The British lost 250 men and seven tanks in withering German fire.

At the same time, the Canadian 2nd Armoured Brigade had been launched against Mohnke's regiment. The brunt of the attack fell on the divisional pioneer battalion, which was now holding the line south of Norrey-en-Bessin. A regiment of Shermans rolled forward, loaded with infantrymen on their rear decks. The pioneers were soon locked in fierce hand-to-hand combat. Shermans were stalked by German Panzerfaust teams through village streets and country lanes.

A Panzer IV company was moved forward from a reserve position to a hill which overlooked the Canadian line of advance. Hitting the Canadians in the flank, some 46 Shermans were soon burning fiercely in the

Normandy fields. Not surprisingly, Shermans were soon nicknamed Ronsons, after the wartime cigarette lighter, because of their alarming ability to burn.

The Panzers now charged the confused mass of Canadians, sending them running back to their start line. Almost 200 Germans were killed or wounded, along with three tanks destroyed, in the desperate battle.

As this battle was taking place, the 40th Canadian Armoured Regiment, along with a commando unit, were launched against the village of Rots, which was at that point held by a composite Kampfgruppe of divisional escort troops and a company of Panthers. Although more than 15 Shermans were knocked out, ultimately the attackers were far too strong for the defenders. They slowly fell back through the streets of the village, inflicting more than 100 casualties on the Allies as they went.

By nightfall, the Canadians were in complete control of the village. During the fighting, just under 70 Germans were killed or wounded, and one Panther tank was knocked out.

In four days of bitter fighting the *Hitlerjugend* Division had effectively brought the Allied advance to a halt on the outskirts of Caen. For a unit in action for the first time, it had put up a remarkable performance. Although many *Hitlerjugend* troopers were despondent that they had not driven the Allies back into the sea, given the odds they faced, they had achieved far more than could be expected. Caen had been Montgomery's objective for the attacks on 7 and 8 June, but the city remained firmly in German hands. The Allied commander would soon try different tactics to take it. One result of the fighting for Caen was a realization by Hitler and the High Command that Normandy was in fact the main Allied invasion front. After Caen, the Führer was finally forced to agree to change his tactics, and accordingly he ordered the *Leibstandarte* Division to move up to the front from its base in Belgium.

Similarly, II SS Panzer Corps was recalled from the Eastern Front on 12 June in order to assist its comrades in their efforts to counter the Allied invasion.

## War criminals on trial

The fighting which took place in the fields and villages to the northwest of Caen was some of the most violent and brutal to be seen during the Normandy campaign. The *Hitlerjugend* Division lost over 1000 dead, wounded or missing in these engagements, while the Canadians alone lost nearly 3000 of their men. Equipment losses were equally heavy on both sides. In those violent first engagements between the *Hitlerjugend* and Canadian troops, little quarter was ever given. As a result, in the bloody aftermath, accusations flew back and forth that many prisoners had been executed by both sides.

Meyer and a number of his officers were charged with war crimes after the war had ended. Meyer was charged with being responsible for five incidents on 7 and 8 June which involved the deaths of 41 Canadian prisoners. He was also charged with issuing orders to his division to give no quarter to prisoners. Seven other *Hitlerjugend* Division officers were investigated for war crimes, involv-

> *In the bloody aftermath, accusations flew back and forth that prisoners were executed by both sides*

ing the deaths of at least 134 Canadian prisoners. After long trials and appeals, Meyer and two others were found guilty of all or some of the charges and sentenced to death. Meyer later had his death sentence stayed, but his two comrades were not so lucky and they faced the hangman's noose in 1948. On his release, Meyer launched a campaign to clear his reputation as well as redeem that of his beloved *Hitlerjugend* Division.

Both sides produced accounts of the unlawful killing of prisoners, the Waffen-SS men claiming that they were subjected to "victor's justice" in show trails. In one famous case, men of the *Hitlerjugend* claimed that they had executed 3 Canadians in reprisal for the deaths of 10 German soldiers tied to a British armoured car and machine-gunned. The truth of these events will never be known, but bear testimony to the fact that during the summer of 1944, Normandy had become a brutal killing field.

■ *Right:* The *Hitlerjugend* Division held the line north of Caen, but at a terrible price in both men and equipment.

# CHAPTER 5

# VILLERS-BOCAGE

## The exploits of Germany's top panzer ace, Michael Wittmann.

With the Canadians and British stalemated in front of Caen by the stalwart defence of the *Hitlerjugend* Division, General Montgomery decided to exploit the gap in the German front. He resolved that this would best be done on the exposed Waffen-SS division's left flank. The *Panzer Lehr* Division was moving into place next to the *Hitlerjugend* after something of a long delay, but in turn its left flank was also exposed, and the Germans had not yet been able to establish a continuous front between the divisions shielding Caen and units fighting the Americans in the western part of Normandy.

Montgomery's answer was Operation Perch. The fresh British 7th Armoured Division was launched southwards around the open left flank of the *Panzer Lehr* Division on 12 June. Its mission was to out-flank the *Panzer Lehr*, then swing around behind it and drive hell for leather through Villers-Bocage towards Caen, trapping both the *Hitlerjugend* and *Panzer Lehr* Divisions. On paper, the plan was very sound; indeed, it was straight out of the Blitzkrieg school of tactics. The execution was flawed, however, and the famous Desert Rats soon found their nemesis in the shape of a single, determined Waffen-SS Tiger I tank commander.

The 55-tonne (54-ton) Tiger I tank had been in service with the Waffen-SS since late 1942. It had first seen action with devastating effect during the heavy fighting around Kharkov on the Eastern Front in February and March 1943. With its 88mm cannon, the Tiger could easily punch through the armour of Soviet T-34s and

■ *Left:* A Tiger I tank of the 101st SS Heavy Panzer Battalion on its way to the Normandy Front to counter the Allied invasion.

Allied Shermans at more than 1500m (1640yd) range. At first the *Leibstandarte*, *Das Reich* and *Totenkopf* Divisions had each been assigned a Tiger I company of some 15 tanks, although the Tiger's notorious unreliability meant that it was often the case that only half of a company's tanks were operational at any one time. These tanks had been used as spearhead units during the Battle of Kursk in July 1943.

As a result of the expansion of the Waffen-SS panzer corps in the summer of 1943, it was decided to remove the divisional Tiger companies and form two corps-level heavy tank battalions. These were nominally to have three Tiger I companies, each with

*The Tiger's unreliability meant that only half a company's tanks were operational at any one time*

14 tanks each. The continued commitment of the *Leibstandarte*, *Das Reich* and *Totenkopf* on the Eastern Front through the winter of 1943, and into the spring of 1944, meant the two new battalions were not ready for action until just before the invasion of France. The 101st SS Heavy Panzer Battalion itself was assigned to support I SS Panzer Corps, and the 102nd SS Heavy Panzer Battalion worked for the sister corps. They were to provide each of the Waffen-SS corps with a hard-hitting strike force, or a reserve counter-punch.

The 101st SS Battalion had been ordered to Normandy immediately after the Allied invasion, but persistent Allied air raids

■ *Below:* Allied bombing of the French railway and bridge networks meant that Waffen-SS Tigers had to drive from Paris to the front, putting a great strain on the vehicles' temperamental tracks and transmissions.

delayed the advance of its 37 operational tanks. It arrived in I SS Panzer Corps' sector west of Caen on 12 June, just as the *Panzer Lehr* Division was taking up position alongside the *Hitlerjugend* Division.

One of its companies, under the command of 30-year-old SS-Oberstürmführer Michael Wittmann, was posted behind the army division and was to be used only as a reserve force. Wittmann was, by June 1944, one of the most highly decorated German tank commanders of the war, boasting the Knight's Cross with Oak Leaves. His kill tally ran to an astronomical 119 tanks, almost all of which were claimed during a particularly successful year serving with the *Leibstandarte*'s Tiger company on the Eastern Front.

Operation Perch got under way during the afternoon of 12 June, with the 22nd Armoured Brigade leading the way. All went well until a single German antitank gun knocked out a British Stuart tank near the village of Livery. Rather than pressing on to exploit the open German flank during the light summer evening, the British commander, Major-General Bobby Erskine, chose to halt for the night. This was turning into no British Blitzkrieg.

## Wittmann on the rampage

Suitably rested, the 7th Armoured Division started out for Villers-Bocage at first light on 13 June and, by 08:00 hours, its advance guard – the task of which had been assigned to the Cromwell tanks of the 4th City of London Yeomanry "Sharpshooters" (4 CLY) – was passing through the town. Another tank unit, the 5th Royal Tank Regiment, a motorized infantry battalion from the Rifle Brigade, as well as assorted antitank and artillery, were in or around the small Norman town ·under the command of the 22nd Armoured Brigade. 4 CLY's A Squadron halted on a prominent hill feature to the east of the town in order to have a rest and brew some tea!

Watching from a nearby wood was Wittmann, who famously replied when he heard his gunner, Bobby Woll's, comment, "they are acting as if they've won the war already" with the retort: "We're going to prove them wrong."

Wittmann ordered his remaining operational Tigers and a Panzer IV from the *Panzer Lehr* Division to stay behind in their hide while he went on a quick reconnaissance mission into the town. He moved south of the British column which was strung out along the Caen road and, unobserved, was able to penetrate into the town. Four Cromwell tanks of the 4 CLY headquarters troop were parked in the main street, with their crews dismounted, making tea or carrying out minor repairs. Wittmann caught them totally by surprise and three of the British tanks were immediately destroyed as he rampaged along the street. One of the tanks was saved by a quick-thinking driver who slammed his vehicle into reverse and backed into a garden.

■ *Above:* Michael Wittmann was soon to become the most famous Tiger tank commander in the Waffen-SS for his exploits at Villers-Bocage.

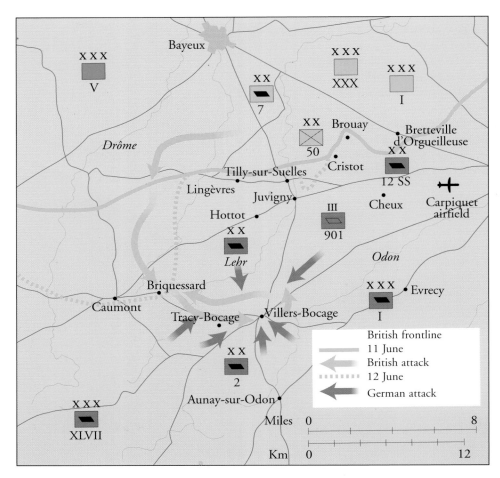

Cruising down the main street of the town, Wittmann drove past this tank and soon found himself confronted by the whole of 4 CLY's B Squadron. After exchanging several shots with the British tanks, including a 17-pounder-armed Sherman Firefly, Wittmann backed off, reversing away and then turning around. His intention was to rejoin his other Tigers but, driving back down the main street, Wittmann found himself head-to-head with the surviving Cromwell tank that had come out to fight him. The two tanks traded rounds at almost point-blank range. Two British 75mm rounds bounced off the front of Wittmann's Tiger, until one of Woll's 88mm shells found its mark, destroying the British tank. Running short of ammunition, Wittmann pulled back and rejoined the rest of his company. After they had re-stocked on 88mm rounds, the company set upon the 4 CLY's A Squadron with a vengeance.

Unobserved by the British, Wittmann's Tigers were able to approach their unsuspecting prey from behind. First of all, they knocked out a M3 halftrack at the rear of the British column. This decisive action effectively trapped the British in a sunken road where, unable to move, their tanks and a range of other vehicles were little more than sitting ducks to their German attackers.

After first dealing with the Sherman Fireflys – which alone could threaten the Tigers – Wittmann's tank, helped by the Panzer IV, just drove along the column, picking off the enemy's vehicles one by one.

> ## *Wittmann found himself head-to-head with the surviving Cromwell that had come out to fight*

By 10:30 hours, the 4 CLY battle group had virtually ceased to exist. The surviving troops on Point 213 surrendered at 13:00 hours.

Wittmann alone had accounted for 23 armoured vehicles, out of a total kill of 20 Cromwells, 4 Sherman Fireflys, 3 Stuarts, 3 artillery observer tanks, 16 Bren Gun carriers, 14 M3 halftracks and 2 6-pounder anti-tank guns. More than 100 British soldiers had been captured and some 62 had been killed. The commanding officer of the 4 CLY, the Viscount Cranley, was later found to be hiding in a wood when German infantry swept the area for prisoners, and he too was captured.

As his tanks were finishing off A Squadron, Wittmann now decided to go after the remainder of the British force in Villers-Bocage itself. 4 CLY's remaining B Squadron had responded to calls for help from its comrades trapped on Point 213, but its men had found the route blocked by the knocked-out Cromwells and a steep railway embankment. A troop of four Cromwells and a Sherman Firefly were then sited in an ambush position in the main square in order to trap any German tanks that might try to push down the main street again for a second attack. A 6-pounder antitank gun was also positioned to fire into the side armour of any tanks which were seen to be driving past the square of the town.

## The British strike back

Unaware of the "Tiger trap" that had been set for him, Wittmann set off into the town, with one of his Tigers and the Panzer IV in close support. The British tanks let Wittmann's Tiger pass by, then the 6-pounder opened up, striking the armoured monster in its vulnerable side armour. A Cromwell got the following Tiger with a similar shot and British infantry with PIAT bazookas opened up as well. The Panzer IV decided to beat a hasty retreat and, blasting at houses known to contain British infantry

■ *Below:* British Cromwell tanks of the 7th Armoured Division were out-gunned and out-armoured by the Waffen-SS Tigers. The Cromwell's main armament was a 75mm gun.

■ *Above:* French
civilians turned out
in their hundreds to
welcome the tanks
of the 7th Armoured
Division as they
pushed south
towards Villers-
Bocage, and a major
defeat.

as it went, the tank turned and retreated at
full speed down the main street of the town.

At this point the Sherman Firefly pulled
out of the square and planted a 17-pounder
shell in the engine of the escaping Panzer IV.
The German crews bailed out of their tanks
and took cover in the now-ruined street. In
the ensuing confusion, they were able to
make good their escape. To prevent the
Germans from recovering their damaged
tanks in order to use them later on in the
conflict, British troops stuffed petrol-soaked
blankets in the tanks' vision ports and set
them on fire.

Wittmann now walked more than 7km
(4.3 miles) to the headquarters of the *Panzer
Lehr* Division. At these headquarters, he
briefed the divisional operations officer on
the action in Villers-Bocage. He was given
command of a company of 15 Panzer IVs
and ordered to clear the town of all British
troops.

The remainder of Wittmann's tanks – as
well as other Tigers from 101st Battalion's
1st Company – had already joined in the
fight when he arrived back at the town at
about 13:00 hours. The 1st Company Tigers
led the attack into the main street of the

town. In the meantime, a Kampfgruppe of infantry from the *Panzer Lehr* Division joined the attack.

British infantry had now reinforced the town and, at the mercy of this strengthened force, the German tanks were met by a hail of PIAT bazooka rounds. Antitank grenades – which the British dropped from upper storeys – were to account for at least one of the four Tigers and one Panzer IV destroyed in the battle.

The Tigers which had survived the battle now pulled back, with this action leaving the remainder of the fighting to the *Panzer Lehr* infantry. By 17:00 hours, an exhausted General Erskine gave the order for the 22nd Brigade to pull out of Villers-Bocage. The battered remnants of this force were to take up their positions on a hill to the east. However, they were given no respite and were pressed closely during the night by the German troops. By the following morning, the Germans had severely dented the British force's morale and had managed to inflict more than 100 casualties.

The Germans continued to press forward, with the 101st SS Battalion's Tigers supporting elements of the 2nd Panzer

> ## By the following morning, the Germans had managed to inflict more than 100 casualties

Division. The men of these units were now arriving in accordance with orders, determined to give their full support to their comrades on the Normandy Front.

## Desert Rats withdraw

A full-scale withdrawal of the 7th Armoured Division was now ordered by a panicked Montgomery. The commander was haunted by visions of his once élite division being cut off behind German lines where it would be left to an uncertain fate. Accordingly, at 14:00 hours, more than 300 RAF heavy bombers started raining 1727 tonnes (1700 tons) of bombs on Villers-Bocage to cover the withdrawal of the Desert Rats. A total count of one Waffen-SS Tiger was destroyed and three damaged in this massive airborne raid. The action would also leave 29 Tiger crews as casualties.

Still the Germans pressed the retreating British and, when the 2nd Panzer's reconnaissance battalion hit the 7th Armoured in the flank, Erskine called in fire from 160 British and American heavy guns to allow his men to break contact. One Tiger was knocked out in this fighting. By nightfall on 14 June, the 7th Armoured Division was

■ *Below:* **The path of Wittmann's Tiger in the main street of Villers-Bocage.**

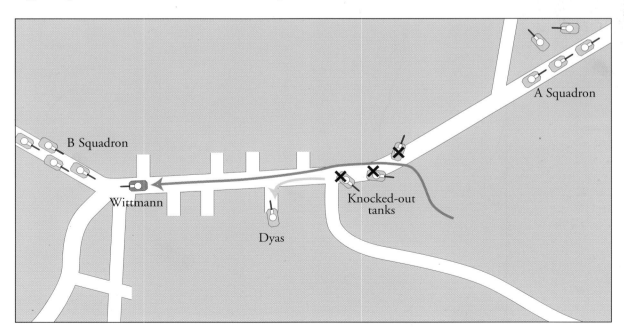

B Squadron

A Squadron

Wittmann

Dyas

Knocked-out tanks

■ *Right:* Wittmann's brief foray into Villers-Bocage left a trail of devastation.

■ *Below:* German armour fell victim to British antitank guns in the village's confined streets.

back at its start-line of two days earlier. It would go down in the annals of history as the unit which suffered the first major Allied defeat of the entire Normandy campaign.

Instead of being a Blitzkrieg, Operation Perch had ended as a shambolic retreat. The materiel losses on the British side were not great and numbered less than 50 tanks. However, during the action, a whole divisional attack had first been thwarted and then decisively thrown back.

Credit for this achievement must surely go to Wittmann, who saw the danger posed by the 22nd Armoured Brigade and was responsible for striking the decisive blow. It was his intervention which gave the *Panzer Lehr* Division's commander – the

redoubtable Fritz Bayerlein – the time he needed to mobilize the counterattack force which was eventually strong enough to drive back the famous Desert Rats.

## Getting Rommel out of Caen

In recognition of his efforts during Operation Perch, on the recommendation of Bayerlein, Wittmann was rewarded with Swords to his Knight's Cross by a grateful Führer. The celebrated Waffen-SS officer was also promoted to the rank of SS-Hauptsturmführer. Smarting in his field headquarters, Montgomery was now preoccupied with devising his next offensive to prise Rommel's men out of Caen. The *Hitlerjugend* would again be the target.

■ *Above:* **To cover the Desert Rats' withdrawal, RAF heavy bombers pummelled Villers-Bocage, causing massive damage but inflicting only a handful of casualties on the remaining Germans. This Cromwell was knocked out by the Germans.**

# CHAPTER 6

# PANZER INFERNO

## The defeat of Operation Epsom and the recapture of Hill 112.

**W**ith the blunting of the outflanking movement by the British 7th Armoured Division at Villers-Bocage, General Montgomery had to look again at how he was going to take Caen, and open a route for his armour to break out into the French countryside beyond. The arrival of the *Panzer Lehr* and 2nd Panzer Divisions in the German frontline to the west of Caen effectively closed down the option of any rapid movement by tank forces out of the Allied bridgehead. Any attack would have to punch straight through the German front.

Montgomery now came up with the idea of a corps-level attack. In this manoeuvre, three infantry divisions backed by enormous fire-power would create a breach for the newly arrived 11th Armoured Division to exploit. More than 60,000 men, backed by more than 600 tanks and 900 guns, would be thrown into the attack. The objective would be the high ground to the west of Caen, just south of the River Odon. This would be the biggest Allied offensive in Normandy so far.

The Allied bridgehead in Normandy was now firmly secure, with thousands of ships delivering 35,000 men, 6000 vehicles and 25,401 tonnes (25,000 tons) of stores a day onto the French coast. By 17 June there were 557,000 Allied troops, with 81,000 vehicles – including 3200 tanks – ashore. The Germans were also racing to reinforce their armies in Normandy. By mid-June 1944, though, Rommel probably only had half as many men at the front as the Allies and some 859 armoured vehicles.

■ *Left:* A German ammunition dump explodes during an RAF attack, further reducing the ability of Rommel to hold his front together.

■ *Above:* RAF
Typhoons operating
from forward
airbases in
Normandy prowled
over German
frontlines, making
any kind of
movement in
daylight very
hazardous.

■ *Left:* German
communications
links, such as the
Paris marshalling
yards, were
devastated by Allied
air raids, making it
impossible for
reinforcements and
supplies to reach
the Normandy Front.

■ *Right:* French
resistance fighters
joined the Allied air
effort to interdict
German lines of
communications.

Aware that the Allies were concentrating on pumping huge amounts of men and materiel ashore into their bridgehead, the German commanders, Rommel and Rundstedt, were constantly engaged in their efforts to muster a strong counterattack force to drive the British and Americans back into the sea.

Great hopes were now placed in the fresh divisions of Paul Hausser's II SS Panzer Corps. This unit was currently *en route* from the Russian Front, and was expected to be available in Normandy in the last week of June 1944.

At the same time, the *Leibstandarte* Division was also – at last – on its way to the front from Belgium, and *Das Reich* and the 17th SS Panzergrenadier Divisions were moving northwards from Toulouse and Bordeaux respectively. It was intended to launch Hausser's corps at the boundary between the British and American bridge-

■ *Right:* The Allies built artificial ports, called Mulberry Harbours, to speed the unloading of supplies into the Normandy bridgehead.

heads. This move would split the Allies apart and the Germans would then be able to crush each of them in turn.

The German plans, however, were constantly being thwarted by the late arrival of the armour necessary for this job. There was also a lack of infantry, which was needed to allow the panzer divisions already in the line to be pulled back and launched into the counterattack.

It was for these reasons that the few panzer divisions which were stationed in Normandy, such as the *Hitlerjugend*, were still holding the front west of Caen a week after being committed to action. Under a relentless bombardment by hundreds of guns, battleship broadsides and thousands of fighter-bombers, German combat power was being steadily wasted away. The *Hitlerjugend's* commander, Fritz Witt, succumbed to a naval gunfire barrage on 14 June when his command post was blasted by a huge salvo. Caught by shell splinters as he dived into a bunker, Witt was killed instantly. The 32-year-old Kurt Meyer was immediately appointed in Witt's place, making him the youngest German divisional commander of the war.

Allied bombing of the French railway and bridge network played havoc with Rommel's attempts to bolster his battered front. The only safe way to move men and materiel by rail was under the cover of darkness, and the nearest railheads to the Normandy Front were a good day's drive away, in the western suburbs of Paris. This geographical constraint posed a particular problem for panzer units which had to make long road-marches to the front from railheads, since it put an immense strain on the sensitive tracks, engines and transmissions of their tanks. The damage caused by this rough ride forced many tanks to be left behind, from where they would be collected by their recovery parties.

These were losses that Rommel's small panzer force could ill-afford. As the panzers approached the front, they started to receive attention from Allied fighter-bombers, the dreaded "Jabos", as they were called by the

> ### Allied bombing played havoc with Rommel's attempts to bolster his battered front

Germans. As an average, German units lost between 5 percent and 10 percent of their vehicle strength to Allied air attacks or mechanical breakdowns as they moved to Normandy. When the *Leibstandarte* arrived at the front in late June, its panzer battalions had only 75 percent of their tanks fit to fight.

Farther from the front, the activities of the French resistance – blowing up bridges and ambushing isolated German columns – were beginning to play a major part in delaying the arrival of Waffen-SS units. Forced by damage to the railway network to travel mainly by road, the *Das Reich* Division was plagued by resistance attacks. However, the division was hardened by years of fighting in Russia and its officers responded in the way they had in the East: brutally, and without any mercy.

## SS retribution

When the *Das Reich* reconnaissance battalion entered the town of Tulle, it allegedly found the remains of 62 German soldiers who had been mutilated, it was claimed, by some resistance fighters. This act of brutality

was said to have taken place after the Germans had surrendered. In response, the *Das Reich* troopers rounded up 99 Frenchmen and hung them from lamp-posts as an example of what would happen if German troops were attacked.

If deterring others was the intention, it failed. Resistance attacks continued apace. Matters came to a head when a *Das Reich* convoy was fired upon near the town of Oradour, killing an SS-Hauptsturmführer. As revenge, the Waffen-SS men ringed the town, rounding up its entire population in the local church, before setting the church on fire. The blaze killed the 548 men, women and children inside the church. One German was killed when a slate fell off a roof and hit him on the head. In the hours that followed, every building in the town was either blown up or set on fire.

This massacre at Oradour was the worst incident of its type in the West to be committed by Waffen-SS troops, although such brutal behaviour was considered routine in the East. Rommel, who had never served in the East, was outraged at the massacre and

■ *Below:* This map shows the German plan to drive a wedge between US and British forces in Normandy, and Montgomery's plan to take Caen, codenamed Operation Epsom. Of the two plans, the British one stood more chance of success given Allied air superiority and their massive materiel advantages.

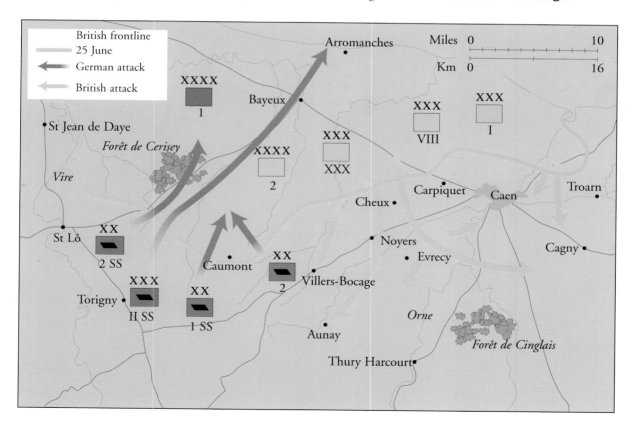

■ *Right:* German logistics could barely cope with moving troops to Normandy, let alone building up the supplies needed to drive the Allies back into the sea.

■ *Above:* Waffen-SS troops prepare for battle as the Normandy campaign begins to reach its climax.

■ *Left:* Tiger II tanks of the army's 503rd Heavy Panzer Battalion arrived at the Normandy Front in mid-July.

during a conference with Hitler, demanded that a number of *Das Reich* officers be punished. The main culprit during the massacre, SS-Sturmbannführer Otto Dickmann, was later killed in action in Normandy, and after his death the Waffen-SS leadership was able to quickly hush up the incident.

Eventually 21 rank-and-file soldiers were put on trial by the French after the war, but it was soon revealed that these men had merely been conscripts from the French-speaking Alsace region, and consequently they were able to persuade the court that

they were unwilling participants. After the war, the French did not rebuild the town, and it stands today as a monument to the suffering of the French victims who died there in 1944.

One week into the invasion, the Germans seemed to be losing the reinforcement race. That was, until mother nature came to Rommel's assistance on 19 June. From that date, four days of storms raged in the Channel, with the result that two of the Allied prefabricated Mulberry harbours were smashed and some 700 ships were run ashore. The arrival of Allied reinforcements dropped to barely a trickle. Only some 9000 men a day were coming ashore and 142,247 tonnes (140,000 tons) of supplies were stranded, backed up in various depots throughout England.

Montgomery's plan for Operation Epsom had to be put back until the last week of June. During Hitler's only ever visit to the Normandy front on 17 June, he ordered Rommel to prepare a massive counterattack. This would involve six panzer divisions, which would be tasked with smashing the Allied bridgehead. Until four of these divisions arrived in the last week of June, all the "Desert Fox" could do was hang on. Whichever side struck first would have a decisive advantage.

■ *Above:* Many German units in Normandy relied on captured vehicles, such as the H39 self-propelled 105mm howitzer based on a Hotchkiss chassis, to augment their firepower.

Montgomery was first off the mark, launching Operation Epsom on 25 June. This was aimed at punching through the forward positions of the *Hitlerjugend* Division. Lieutenant-General Sir Richard O'Connor's VIII Corps commanded the offensive, while the 49th, 15th and 43rd Infantry Divisions were responsible for taking the lead in the advance.

The 11th Armoured Division was held in reserve close behind the front, ready go into action once crossings over the Odon River had been seized. Its objective was Hill 112, which dominated a swathe of the Norman countryside to the west of Caen. The gentle slopes of the hill were covered in open cornfields that provided superb fields of fire for the German gunners who were engaged in defending it. Meyer, Dietrich and Rommel correctly judged that whoever held the hill would control Caen, and with it Normandy, and they all resolved that no effort would be spared keeping it.

The British attack was sequenced, with the 146th and 147th Infantry Brigades hitting Wilhelm Mohnke's 26th Panzergrenadier Regiment at 05:00 hours. Heavy

> ## The 901st Panzergrenadiers broke under the pressure and were relieved by the Hitlerjugend *panzers*

fog covered the battlefield, making it impossible for the German defenders to strike the British infantry before they were almost on top of their positions.

Heavy fighting surged around the village of Fontenay-le-Pesnel and the nearby Tessel woods. Two companies of Panzer IVs were called up to lead a counterattack, which stabilized the situation. However, the neighbouring 901st Panzergrenadier Regiment broke under the pressure, and had to be relieved by the panzers of the *Hitlerjugend* Division By nightfall Fontenay village itself was still being fought over, with Waffen-SS men holding out in a string of strongpoints. The *Hitlerjugend* panzers, however, still managed to hold the high ground near the village of Rauray, and this vantage point was to play a crucial part in the forthcoming battle.

During the night, the commander of the *Hitlerjugend*'s Panzer Regiment, Max Wünsche, was ordered to form a Kampfgruppe to throw back the 49th Division's penetration into Fontenay. Just as the *Hitlerjugend* Panzer IVs and Panthers were advancing into the dawn, British

Shermans of the 24th Lancers and 4th/7th Dragoon Guards were also starting to roll forward into the attack from the eastern edge of the village. A fierce tank battle was developing in the fields south of the village when Meyer, who was watching from Rauray with Wünsche, started to receive reports that a major British attack was developing against the division's centre. He immediately called off the panzer attack and began moving troops to counter the new threat.

It was now the turn of the 15th Highland Division to attack. At exactly 07:30 hours, 700 guns started blasting the positions of the *Hitlerjugend* pioneer battalion around the village of St Manvieu. For 10 minutes this storm of destruction laid waste fields, villages and woods. Then the barrage started to move forward at a rate of 100m (9144yd) every three minutes. Behind this torrent of fury came two brigades of British infantry, walking with fixed bayonets. This neatly scheduled attack soon broke down into chaos when nine British Shermans exploded in a minefield laid by the pioneers. Nevertheless, despite furious resistance from the pioneers, they were just overwhelmed.

*Behind the torrent of fury came two brigades of British infantry walking with fixed bayonets*

By late morning the British had pushed 3km (1.8 miles) through the *Hitlerjugend* lines, and had captured Cheux. This success was far from easily won: the assaulting regiments had each lost more than 100 men. Several British tanks were victims of Panzerfaust fire in these actions, but nonetheless it seemed that the British armour had opened a way through to the Odon. Three armoured regiments were able to cruise on forward.

However, Meyer had not finished his work yet. He ordered all of his available tanks to move to cover the breach in the line. Panzer IVs were posted in ambush positions facing eastwards on the high ground at Rauray, and Panthers moved in from their reserve positions at Carpiquet airfield in order that they might hit the British from the other flank. Both sides were poised for battle.

Dietrich now released Tigers of the 101st SS Heavy Panzer Battalion and assault guns of the 21st Panzer Division. Numbers of 88mm Flak batteries were also mustered to form an antitank gun line ahead of the British tanks. All through the afternoon and

■ *Above:* Waffen-SS antitank units in Normandy fielded large numbers of Marder III self-propelled guns.

■ *Above:* Flail tanks of the British 79th Armoured Divisions were used to clear paths through German minefields.

into the evening, the German panzer crews and Flak gunners duelled with the British tank crews.

As night fell, some 50 British tanks could be seen through the darkness, burning around Cheux. Meyer's desperate measure had just held the line. Some panzers had even managed to fight their way into St Manvieu and rescue groups of pioneers engaged in fighting behind the British lines. German losses were grievous, though. The *Hitlerjugend* Division lost more than 750 dead, wounded or missing, some 325 taken from the pioneer battalion.

Montgomery and O'Connor now made the decision to pile on the pressure even more and ordered that the 43rd Wessex Division be fed into the battle, allowing the 15th Division to push its 227th Highland Brigade forward through Cheux to make a dash for the Odon. The 4th Armoured Brigade was brought up to roll behind the

infantry, and was awarded the responsibility of leading the breakout.

Blocking the British axis of advance between Grainville-sur-Odon and Marcelet was a Kampfgruppe made up of 30 Panzer IVs and a number of StuG III assault guns. Based around Rauray were 17 Panthers of the *Hitlerjugend*'s 1st Panzer Battalion, backed by a dozen 101st Battalion Tigers. Holding the Odon were a number of 88mm batteries. A Panther company from the 2nd Panzer Division was also dispatched to help Meyer hold the line. Groups of pioneers and panzergrenadiers had turned many of the villages along the Odon into well-fortified strongpoints, but Meyer's defence plan relied on the long-range killing power of his many panzer and Flak guns.

The British attack got off to a slow start because Cheux was clogged with troops, tanks and supply vehicles. This chaos was not helped by the fact that the 2nd Panzer

Division's Panthers made an unauthorized attack and that its move was beaten back, with the loss of 4 out of its 17 tanks.

A weak attack in the morning by one Scottish regiment was easily defeated by the panzers covering Rauray. Early in the afternoon, a strong force of Scottish infantry of the Argylls backed by the 23rd Hussars pushed south towards the Odon. Shermans duelled with Panthers, Tigers and Panzer IVs all through the day.

The *Hitlerjugend*'s weak infantry strength meant that it was not able to establish a continuous front along the wooded river valley, which allowed the Argylls to find an undefended route to a bridge. Just after 22:00 hours, the first tanks of the 23rd Hussars were across the Odon and fanning out towards Hill 112. Meyer heard that his

vital ground was under threat when his radio interception unit picked up triumphant radio conversations from the British tanks as they advanced, apparently unopposed, from the Argylls' bridgehead at Mandrainville. Overnight the British 159th Brigade joined the Argylls, and elements of the 29th Armoured Brigade were also across the Odon, accompanied by more than 150 Sherman tanks.

## Holding Hill 112

During the night, Meyer had resorted to desperate measures to rush reinforcements to hold Hill 112. The strongpoints at Rauray and Marcelet were abandoned to release a company of Panzer IVs and panzergrenadiers, as well as an 88mm battery from the Luftwaffe. They reached the summit

■ *Below:* Churchill tanks of the 7th Royal Tank Regiment were in the forefront of Operation Epsom, supporting British infantry as they cleared Normandy villages of *Hitlerjugend* panzergrenadiers.

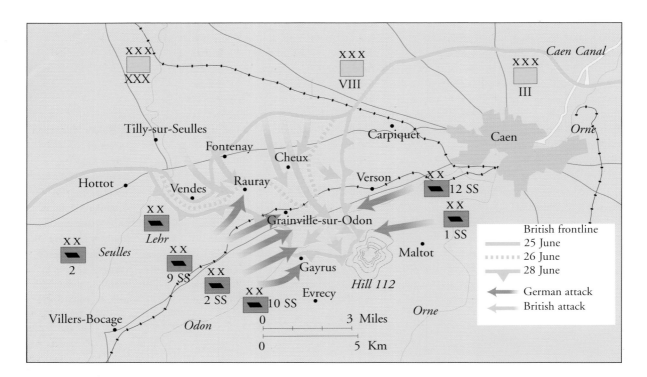

British frontline
— 25 June
···· 26 June
▼ 28 June
← German attack
← British attack

■ *Above:* **Operation Epsom was not a success, largely due to the fanatical resistance offered by the Waffen-SS panzer divisions.**

during the night and were ready and waiting when the British tanks began moving forward at dawn on 28 June. British tanks were soon burning on the slopes of the hill. However, in response, RAF Typhoon strike aircraft were called in to rocket the German tanks, enabling the British infantry to start edging forward, gradually outflanking the outnumbered panzergrenadiers. By noon the Germans had been pushed off the exposed summit of the hill.

Wünsche was soon on the scene and set about mustering the remains of his panzer regiment to contain the British breakthrough. Panthers and Panzer IVs were positioned around three sides of the hill in order to pen in the British, who were threatening to overwhelm the thinly stretched defences. The presence of 30 *Hitlerjugend* panzers, backed by 88mm Flak guns and Nebelwerfer rockets, was just enough to hold the line. Three times during the day Wünsche led his tanks forward into a storm of 17-pounder fire from the now dug-in British antitank guns in the woods along the banks of the Odon.

*The* Hitlerjugend *had been in action for 48 hours straight and was falling asleep in its trenches*

The British were still determined to hold Hill 112 whatever the cost, feeding new armoured regiments into the battle until their point units ran out of ammunition or tanks. By the time the last of Wünsche's attacks went in at 17:00 hours, some 40 Shermans were smashed on the slopes of the vital ground. As darkness fell over the battlefield, the British troops had retained their precarious foothold on Hill 112.

Meyer's division was now almost split in two by the huge British penetration. Mohnke's panzergrenadier regiment was just about holding out on the eastern edge of the British salient, and the remainder of the division was stopping O'Connor's tanks from driving directly into Caen from the east. The British were desperate to expand their breach and relentlessly attacked the *Hitlerjugend* positions during 28 June. The *Hitlerjugend* troops had been in action for almost 48 hours straight and were exhausted. Those who were not dead or wounded were falling asleep in their trenches and tank turrets. Help was now desperately needed if the division's front was not to collapse under the pressure.

Just in time, elements of the *Leibstandarte* and *Das Reich* Divisions were approaching the battlefield. They were to be launched in a coordinated attack to pinch off the top of the British salient. Kampfgruppe *Weidinger* from *Das Reich's Der Führer* Panzergrenadier Regiment was thrown in to bolster Mohnke's hard-pressed regiment around Grainville-sur-Odon. With only a handful of army Panthers in support, all Mohnke's Waffen-SS men could do was doggedly hold on to the string of villages along the north bank of the Odon through the day against attacks by a British infantry brigade with strong Churchill tank support.

### The *Leibstandarte*'s attack

On the other side of the salient, which had now been dubbed the "Scottish Corridor", two panzergrenadier battalions of the *Leibstandarte*

*A tank battle developed around Cheux, and by the end of the day 60 British tanks were burning*

entered the battle in a dawn attack from the village of Verson. Dietrich pulled together strong panzer support in the shape of 22 Panzer IVs from the 21st Panzer Division, a company of *Hitlerjugend* Panthers, and three Tigers of the 101st SS Battalion. At first the *Leibstandarte* Kampfgruppe swept all before it, sending the Monmouthshire Regiment reeling back in disorder and destroying three British tanks. The advance continued for another 3km (1.9 miles) until the British defence solidified around Colleville. Then tanks of the British 4th Armoured Brigade were thrown in against the *Leibstandarte*'s flank. In the face of this onslaught and a massive supporting artillery barrage, the German attack faltered. Five Panthers were lost and several other tanks damaged. The *Leibstandarte* spearhead was less than 3km (1.9 miles) from the *Das Reich* troopers in Grainville-sur-Odon. Nevertheless, the Scottish Corridor remained open to Hill 112.

During the morning of 28 June, the German command in Normandy was thrown into crisis by the suicide of Colonel-General Friedrich Dollman, commander of the Seventh Army. Dollman was the senior German officer on the Normandy Front in the absence of Rommel and Rundstedt, who had been summoned to Berchtesgaden for a conference with the Führer.

### Dollman's cyanide

The British seizure of the bridgehead over the Odon had thrown all the German plans for a counterattack against the British bridgehead into chaos. This attack was planned for 29 June with II SS Panzer Corps, which was assembling after its long road march from Paris to the southwest of Caen. At 20:10 hours, Dollman decided that the situation on the *Hitlerjugend*'s front was so precarious that Hausser's corps would have to be diverted for a immediate counter-stroke against the western flank of the British salient. Hausser replied to Dollman that his troops would not be ready to take action for another day.

Dollman was already in a precarious position. He had been placed under investigation by Hitler's lackeys for the loss of Cherbourg to the Americans two days before. Not wanting to face the wrath of the Führer for countermanding his attack orders, the colonel-general reached for his cyanide capsule.

The next most senior German officer in Normandy was Hausser, and within a few hours he had been ordered to replace Dollman. Fearing that it was not a good idea to change command just as his corps was about to attack, Hausser remained with his troops for one more day before handing over to SS-Gruppenführer Willi Bittrich, who was at that time the commander of the *Hohenstaufen* Division.

Throughout the night, Hausser's men were struggling to get into position for an attack at 06:00 hours. With a combined strength of more than 30,000 men, 79 Panthers, 79 Panzer IVs and 76 StuG IIIs, II Panzer Corps was the largest German armoured formation to enter battle *en masse* during the entire Normandy campaign. The corps' Tiger battalion had yet to arrive at the front, so it was unable to offer support for the attack on 29 June.

■ *Above:* Troops of British VIII Corps smashed through the *Hitlerjugend*'s front and raced southwards to the strategic Odon bridges.

■ *Left:* British infantry advance through the corn fields of the Odon valley at the height of the Epsom Offensive.

Alerted by their ULTRA code-breaking operation, the British were well aware of the impending counterattack. Montgomery, fearful of the 11th Armoured Division's tanks being cut off around Hill 112, decided that he would pull back the 4th and 29th Armoured Brigades from the bridgeheads south of the Odon and concentrate his tanks to beat back the German attack on the flanks of the Scottish Corridor. Operation Epsom was halted. His caution at this key moment in the battle gave the Germans a much-needed respite and allowed them to shore up their front once more.

Using his ULTRA intelligence, Montgomery now decided to unleash his artillery and airpower against II SS Panzer Corps. The *Hohenstaufen* and *Frundsberg* Divisions were caught in their assembly areas

around Noyers by huge artillery barrages, then waves of RAF Typhoons swooped down to machine-gun and rocket their columns.

The *Hohenstaufen* was given the objective of Cheux, at the heart of the Scottish Corridor. An attack by 100 RAF Lancaster bombers on one of the division's assembly areas played havoc with its attack and it did not roll forward until the early afternoon. With its two panzergrenadier regiments in the lead, the division quickly secured Grainville-sur-Odon. As the Waffen-SS Panzer IVs, Panthers and StuG IIIs took the lead for the advance on Cheux they ran into the British 4th Armoured Brigade. A swirling tank battle developed around Cheux, and by the end of the day some 60 British tanks were burning in the fields. Some 30 panzers and assault guns were lost

■ *Left:* The commitment of Hausser's II SS Panzer Corps stabilized the Odon Front, but it meant that Hitler's plans for a major counterattack in Normandy had to be shelved permanently.

in this battle, which failed to produce the decisive breakthrough which its tacticians had anticipated.

At the same time, the *Leibstandarte* Kampfgruppe tried to push westwards in order to effect a link-up with the *Hohenstaufen* Division. However, the *Leibstandarte*'s attack never got beyond its start-line: the Waffen-SS troopers had been hit hard by a British armoured regiment. Although the Kampfgruppe did manage to destroy 12 tanks, later on it was forced to retreat and surrender two villages to the British 43rd Division.

■ *Below:* Hill 112 became a vicious killing ground as both sides battled to control its strategic heights.

South of the Odon River, the *Frundsberg* Division was ordered to clear the British from Hill 112 for good. A rocket barrage from 60 Nebelwerfers swept the hill prior to the attack. This time the panzers led the way and the Germans cleared a number of key villages on the southern edge of Hill 112 of British infantry, and knocked out 12 British tanks. Heavy rain lashed the battlefield during the night, but Hausser was not about to give the British any respite. More rocket fire poured down on the hill and the *Frundsberg* pressed home its attacks, assisted by *Hitlerjugend* tanks firing from the southern and eastern slopes. Shortly after dawn, *Frundsberg* and *Hitlerjugend* Panzer IVs were on the summit of Hill 112. Panzergrenadier attackers were then sent forward to mop up the last remaining British bridgeheads over the Odon.

## Aftermath

In five days of bloody fighting, Montgomery almost cracked open the German front in Normandy. Operation Epsom had nearly succeeded, yet at key moments, quick thinking and aggressive defence by Waffen-SS commanders snatched victory from the jaws of defeat. Success came with a price. The *Hitlerjugend* Division was hardest hit, suffering some 1240 casualties. *Hohenstaufen* was hit hard during the Allied air attacks on 29 June, losing 1150 men in a two-day period. *Frundsberg* was not so heavily engaged and lost 570 casualties. Casualty figures for the *Leibstandarte* and *Das Reich* Kampfgruppen are not available. In total, the five Waffen-SS divisions engaged must have lost in excess of 3500 men, compared to 4020 British losses.

While the Germans had halted the British and held their line, their casualties were grievous. Unlike the British, who replaced their losses in a matter of days, the Germans got no replacements to fill their ranks. The Russians had just started a major offensive on the Eastern Front and the Führer decreed that troops in Normandy could expect no relief. General Montgomery may have been outfought by the Waffen-SS in the course of Operation Epsom, but nonetheless he was bleeding Hitler's élite panzer force white. The likes of Rommel, Dietrich and Meyer were beginning to wonder how long their troops would be able to withstand such harsh punishment.

> *Dietrich and Meyer were wondering how long their troops could withstand such punishment*

■ *Above:* British prisoners being escorted to the rear. The retaking of Hill 112 was a brief respite for the German front in Normandy.

91

# CHAPTER 7

# "MAKE PEACE YOU FOOLS"

## The fight to hold the Odon line and Hill 112.

**F**our weeks into the Normandy campaign, Rommel now rec-ommended a tactical withdrawal to a line south of Caen, to pull the hard-pressed troops back out of range of the massive Allied battleship broadsides. Almost 100,000 German soldiers had been killed, injured or captured. Units such as Meyer's *Hitlerjugend* were being bled to death. It alone had lost more than 20 percent of its frontline fighting strength. Only by fighting a mobile battle could the Allies be held in Normandy, or so said the "Desert Fox".

When Rommel's superior, Rundstedt, forwarded his suggestions to Hitler's headquarters, no one was prepared to put the suggestion to the Führer, who was, as usual, demanding that not a metre of land be surrendered to the enemy. When a sheepish Field Marshal Wilhelm Keitel asked for alternative suggestions that could be put to the Führer, Rundstedt made his famous reply: "Make peace, you fools". Within hours, the veteran field marshal was replaced by Hans

■ *Left:* StuG IIIs of II SS Panzer Corps bolstered the defence of Hill 112 as the battle for Normandy dragged on into July 1944.

■ *Above:* Waffen-SS Panthers were held back from the front to provide local reserves to counterattack any Allied breakthroughs.

■ *Right:* Max Wünsche, the commander of the *Hitlerjugend*'s panzer regiment, was put in command of a Kampfgruppe that was the key to the division's defence of Caen.

von Kluge. Born on 30 October 1882, in Posen, Prussia, he was one of Adolf Hitler's ablest commanders on the Eastern Front during World War II.

Of an old aristocratic family, Kluge served in World War I and remained in the army after the war. During World War II he successfully led an army in the Polish, French and early Russian campaigns. As

commander of Army Group Centre, in the Soviet Union from December 1941 until he was wounded in October 1943, he was largely successful in containing the massive Soviet offensives against his forces. After the Allied landings in France in June 1944, Hitler, on 3 July, replaced Field Marshal Gerd von Rundstedt, the German commander-in-chief West, with Kluge, who was unable to stop the Anglo-American advance.

Certainly, Rundstedt could expect no help from Keitel, a field marshal and head of the German armed forces high command. One of Adolf Hitler's most loyal and trusted lieutenants, he became chief of the Führer's personal military staff and helped direct most of the Third Reich's World War II campaigns. Serving mainly as a staff officer in World War I and in administrative posts under the Weimar Republic (1918–33), Keitel became chief of staff of the armed forces office, equivalent to minister of war, in 1935, and in 1938 advanced to be head of the armed forces high command, which Hitler had created as a central control agency for Germany's military effort. In June 1940 Keitel dictated the terms of the French surrender. After the war he was convicted at the

International Military Tribunal at Nuremberg of authorizing the shooting of hostages and other acts, and was executed. He was generally regarded as a weak officer who had little tactical military experience and who served chiefly as Hitler's lackey.

Other officers Hitler considered lacking in "fighting spirit" were also purged from the Normandy Front. Rommel was looking increasingly isolated. He started to canvas senior commanders in France about disobeying the Führer's orders and making a strategic withdrawal. Even hardened Waffen-SS commanders could see the futility of the current strategy. Dietrich was won over and declared to Rommel: "You're the boss, Herr Feldmarschall, I obey only you – whatever it is you are planning."

Suggestions have been made that Rommel was trying to enlist his subordinates in the famous 20 July Bomb Plot to kill Hitler. No firm evidence of this has emerged. Whatever he was planning came to nothing, because on 17 July an RAF Typhoon shot up Rommel's staff car during one of his daily visits to the front. Badly wounded, Rommel was evacuated to Germany and would play no more part in the battle for Normandy or the plot to kill Hitler. Three months later, in the witch-hunt after the bomb plot, Rommel was offered the choice of standing trial or taking his own life. He opted for the poison.

In front of Caen, Montgomery had not given up his ambitions to destroy the Waffen-SS panzer divisions and seize the Norman city. The *Hitlerjugend* Division was still the rock of the German defence, positioned in a semi-circle in its western suburbs. The arrival of II SS Panzer Corps had released Meyer's division from the responsibility of

■ *Below:*
*Hitlerjugend* pioneers in a SdKfz 251/7 armoured halftrack specially modified for combat engineer tasks.

holding the western edge of the Scottish Corridor, and allowed him to concentrate it for the defence of Caen. The 25th Panzergrenadier Regiment was holding the villages to the northwest of the city, and Wilhelm Mohnke's regiment was holding to the west of the city, centred on Carpiquet airfield. Meyer still had a Kampfgruppe from the *Leibstandarte* under his command, and he posted it to the south of the airfield. Max Wünsche's panzers were holding the eastern edges of the Hill 112 feature. It would be mid-July before the *Hitlerjugend*'s sister division would be in Normandy in strength.

The *Frundsberg* Division was firmly entrenched on the summit of Hill 112 and the nearby Hill 113. It was now reinforced by the Tigers of the 102nd SS Heavy Panzer Battalion. Willi Bittrich's other division, the *Hohenstaufen*, was on the north bank of the Odon, linking his corps to the army panzer units to the west.

Dietrich and Bittrich could muster a combined total of 94 Panzer IVs, 45 Panthers, 48 StuG IIIs and just over 30 Tiger Is ready for battle.

## Deploying the divisions

Meyer's tried and battered division based its defences on a series of village strongpoints held by panzergrenadiers, while 88mm Flak guns were deployed covering open ground between the villages, and panzers held back in reserve for counterattacks. Bittrich's stronger divisions were deployed more aggressively, with his Panthers, Tigers and 88mm guns positioned on high ground in order to be able to sweep the approaches to both Hill 112 and Hill 113.

It was now the turn of the Canadians to return to the fray, and they were given the objective of taking the northwestern corner of Caen in Operation Windsor. The attack opened on the evening of 3 July with a massive salvo from the British battleship *Rodney*'s 16in guns. Then some 500 Canadian and British guns opened fire. Shells rained down on Carpiquet airfield throughout the night. At dawn the 8th Canadian Brigade was launched against the airfield. A forward panzergrenadier company held the attack briefly, while panzer reserves were mobilized. As the 17 tanks came up, a *Hitlerjugend* 88mm Flak battery on high ground outside the airfield started to rip into the Canadian tanks. Throughout the day, the Canadians tried to push forward across the airfield's runway, but were rebuffed with heavy losses. RAF Typhoons were called in to blast a route through the defences. No panzers were hit and they kept up a furious resistance, hitting more than a dozen tanks and inflicting almost 400 casualties. To relieve pressure on the troops defending the airfield, a *Leibstandarte* panzergrenadier battalion was moved to its northern edge to launch a night attack. The assault was halted after German artillery fire mistakenly hit the Waffen-SS troopers.

■ *Below:* German armour scatters as American fighter-bombers appear overhead to the northwest of Caen.

## Bombs away

Rebuffed with heavy losses at Carpiquet, Montgomery now decided to call up RAF Bomber Command to blast the *Hiterjugend* out of Caen. During the evening of 7 July, some 467 Lancaster and Halifax heavy bombers dumped 2540 tonnes (2500 tons) of bombs on the city in a raid that turned much of it into rubble. To avoid any of his troops being accidentally hit, Montgomery held back the follow-up infantry assault until 08:00 hours on 8 July. Laudable though this was, it meant Meyer's men had time to recover from the shock of the raid and dust

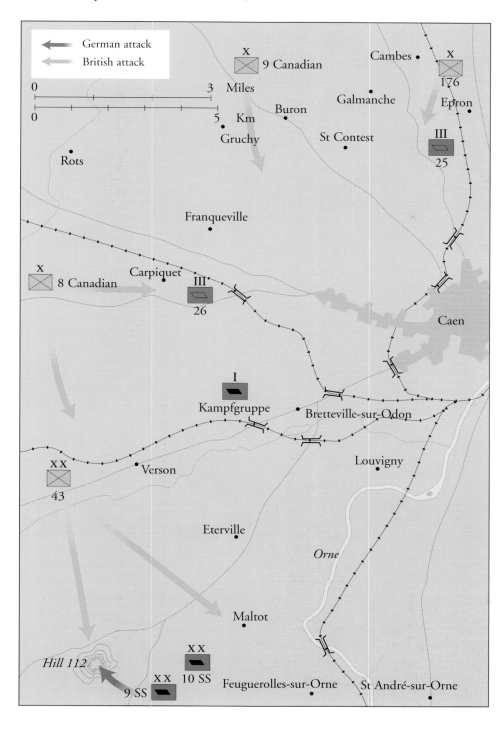

■ *Left:* The *Hitlerjugend*'s defence of Caen cost the division dear. Some 28 percent of its manpower strength was lost.

off their weapons in time to meet the inevitable attack.

## Operation Charnwood

First into the attack during Operation Charnwood was the British 176th Infantry Brigade, which was to seize the northern suburbs of Caen. Then the Canadian 9th Infantry Brigade would take the northwest corner of the city. The defenders were soon on the verge of being overwhelmed. Hand-to-hand fighting raged all day in the villages held by Meyer's troops. Apart from a single company of *Hitlerjugend* Panthers, there were few reserves, and Meyer used them to rescue panzergrenadiers trapped by Canadian attacks. The 32-year-old divisional commander even joined the battle at one

stage, stalking Canadian tanks with a Panzerfaust. Almost 500 *Hitlerjugend* men were killed or wounded during the fighting. Then the Canadians threw in a fresh brigade. Meyer asked Dietrich for permission to withdraw, which was initially refused because it conflicted with a Führer order "to hold to the last bullet". By nightfall, Dietrich relented, and Meyer's battered division was starting to pull back into Caen and across the Orne River to a form a new defensive line, alongside the advance elements of the *Leibstandarte* which was finally arriving in strength. This was just in time. The *Hitlerjugend* Division had lost some 3300 men, or 28 percent of its manpower strength, and half its tanks had been knocked out since it was committed to battle on 6

■ *Above:* RAF Lancaster heavy bombers rained destruction on German positions in Normandy.

■ *Right:* Further aerial firepower was provided by RAF Halifaxes, which joined the daily raids against German positions in Normandy and supply lines else-where in France.

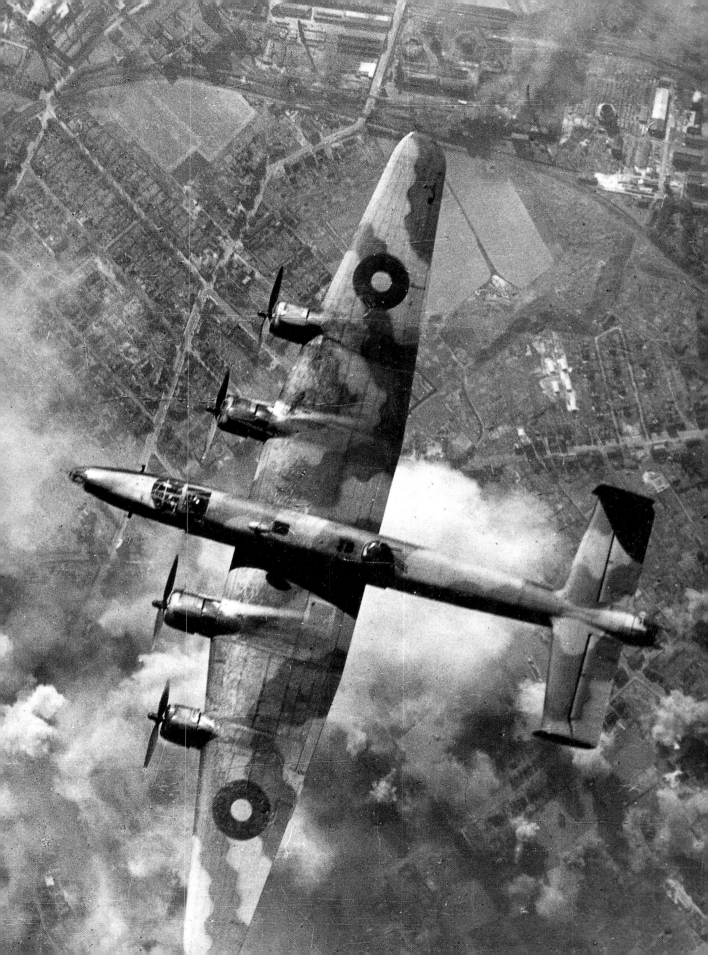

■ **Above:** Rocket-firing RAF Typhoons proved a major headache for German panzer commanders, making it almost impossible to conduct large-scale operations in daylight.

June. Apart from 17 replacement Panther tanks, it had received no men or materiel to fill the breaches in its ranks.

It was now the turn of the divisions of II SS Panzer Corps to feel Montgomery's wrath. The 43rd Wessex Division was given the objective of driving the Germans from Hill 112 once and for all, opening the way for the 4th Armoured Brigade to surge forward and seize crossings over the River Orne. Standing in their way was the *Frundsberg* Division of SS-Brigadeführer Heinz Harmel, reinforced by the pitiful remains of Max Wünsche's *Hitlerjugend* Panzer Regiment.

Operation Jupiter kicked off with the usual heavy artillery barrage, after which two infantry brigades, supported by heavy Churchill infantry tanks, began frontal attacks on Hill 112 and the village of Maltot on its northern slope. As a novelty, the British tried to cover their dawn attack with a huge smoke barrage, which only served to blind their own artillery observers at a key moment in the battle.

Panzergrenadiers duelled with the waves of British infantry, while dug-in 88mm Flak guns picked off a whole regiment's worth of Churchills. When it looked like 25 Churchills were going to take the summit of Hill 112, *Frundsberg's* panzer battalion arrived from its reserve position and "brewed up" most of them. More Churchills were thrown in to support the 129th Infantry Brigade's attack, which was now making ground on the northern slope of the hill. Bittrich then committed his Tigers and rapidly started to tear into the heavily armoured, but under-gunned, British tanks.

The British, fortunately, had some of their 17-pounder antitank guns to hand, and they equalized the battle, knocking out several Tigers. In spite of this, the German defences on the hill were just too strong, and some 43 British tanks burned on its northern slope. The commander of the 43rd Division eventually rescinded orders to commit the 4th Armoured Brigade's last tank regiment after its commander persuaded him they would suffer 75 percent losses.

Simultaneously, as the attack on Hill 112 was going in, the British 130th Brigade was assaulting Maltot. Three regiments of

> *The German defences on the hill were too strong, and 43 British tanks burned on its northern slope*

infantry backed by more Churchills had to attack across open ground to seize their objectives on the northern bank of the Orne River. After making good progress, the brigade was soon being raked by fire from three sides. Tigers of the 102nd SS Battalion on Hill 112 were firing into the British left flank, *Hitlerjugend* Panthers and Panzers IVs were to the attacker's front, and elements of the *Leibstandarte* Kampfgruppe were on the right. The British were caught in a classic killing zone, which knocked out most of the attacking squadron of tanks. Determined infantrymen from the Hampshire and Dorset Regiments made it into Maltot. Harmel rushed to the scene in his armoured command halftrack with the *Frundsberg's* reconnaissance battalion to evict the British infantry. With close support from the Tigers,

all the Dorset Regiment's antitank guns were knocked out and the British soldiers were soon streaming back to their start-line.

Back on Hill 112, the Duke of Cornwall's Light Infantry were launched forward into the attack as dusk was falling, and took the summit at last. A counterattack led by a handful of Tigers failed to dislodge the British from their newly won prize.

With the key to the German position in central Normandy about to fall, Dietrich and Bittrich re-shuffled their forces to strike back. SS-Standartenführer Sylvester Stadler's *Hohenstaufen* Division was released from west of the Odon to counterattack and retake Hill 112. During the night, the division was moved into position on the western slope of the hill ready to attack as soon as its artillery was in position to give supporting

■ *Below:* German armour losses rose steadily during July, and the supply of replacement vehicles was reduced to a trickle by Allied bombing of German supply lines. This is a knocked-out Panzer IV tank.

fire. Congested roads meant the attack was delayed for several hours and when the panzergrenadiers at last started to move forward, they ran into withering artillery barrages. Even the presence of Tigers in the assault wave had failed to make any impression on the British defences by dawn on 11 July. The arrival of daylight gave the German tanks an edge at last and they drove off the British armoured regiment that had moved up to the crest of Hill 112, leaving infantry and 17-pounders to hold it. By the middle of the afternoon the British infantry regiment was being ripped to pieces by machine-gun, tank, artillery, mortar and rocket fire. *Hohenstaufen*'s assault gun battalion led yet one more attack forward, and it swept away the Duke of Cornwall's, leaving 250 dead or wounded behind, including their commanding officer, on the summit of the hill. The

Germans had regained control of Hill 112 and stayed on its summit for the rest of July.

II SS Panzer Corps remained the anchor of the German defence on the Odon line for the remainder of July. On 15 July Montgomery launched Operation Greenline to expand the British front down the Odon valley. Its aim was to keep II SS Panzer Corps occupied while the British massed their armour for a major attack to the east of Caen. In this aim it succeeded. A breakthrough around Noyers forced Bittrich to move the *Hohenstaufen* to close the breach on 16 July. Only some 20 panzers could be mustered to form the assault Kampfgruppe as it attacked from Hill 113 towards the Odon. The panzers ran into a British tank brigade and chased it off, knocking out 48 Shermans and capturing a dozen for the loss of five German tanks. The division was soon

■ *Below:* British infantry and armour outside Caen. Fighting in the hedgerows and villages of Normandy was slow and painful for both sides.

sucked into a meat-grinder battle. A day later its two panzergrenadier regiments had to be combined into a single Kampfgruppe, while its panzer regiment could only muster 25 Panthers, 13 Panzer IVs and 15 StuG IIIs.

## Holding the British at bay

The *Frundsberg* Division remained on Hill 112, fighting off a sustained series of attacks. Almost every day British infantry and tanks tried their luck against the Waffen-SS lines. In just over two weeks of fighting it had lost more than 2200 men. Its panzer regiment was reduced to 12 operational Panzer IVs and 6 StuG IIIs. Only with help from the 102nd SS Battalion's Tigers was the division able to hold the British at bay.

The bitter fighting to the west of Caen had bled II SS Panzer Corps dry, reducing Rommel's last panzer reserve to a shadow of its former self. The last hope for the

Germans was the arrival at last of the *Leibstandarte* Division to the south of Caen. Rommel's brush with death robbed the German Army in Normandy of its commander at a crucial point. The new commander in France, Kluge, had little idea of what was going on at the front, preferring to stay in his chateau near Paris, preoccupying himself with his plot to overthrow Hitler. He would take his own life in August 1944, after Hitler began to suspect he was attempting to negotiate with the Allies.

The Normandy Front was now being largely run by Waffen-SS generals. Hausser commanded the Seventh Army, leading the battle against the Americans, while Bittrich and Dietrich were commanders of the bulk of the German armour fighting Montgomery's armies. In the coming weeks, they would shoulder the responsibility for holding the beleaguered front together.

■ *Above:* Tiger Is proved bulwarks of the German defence in Normandy. However, as this picture shows, they were not immune to Allied bombing.

# CHAPTER 8

# BLUNTING GOODWOOD

## I SS Panzer Corps and the defeat of Montgomery's attack.

**A**s British and Canadian troops inched slowly into the devastated ruins of Caen, General Montgomery was putting the final touches to his next major offensive. This one, he hoped, would crack open the German defences in Normandy once and for all. Montgomery planned to throw in three armoured divisions – with 877 tanks which were to be backed by 10,000 assault infantry and 8000 vehicles – into the fray. The biggest preparatory bombardment so far in the campaign – involving some 712 guns, 942 British and 571 US heavy bombers – would deliver a massive 300,000 shells and some 7823 tonnes (7700 tons) of bombs onto the weaker German defenders.

Operation Goodwood, as the offensive was codenamed, would be launched from the small bridgehead over the Orne River, to the east of Caen, that had been seized in the first hours of D-Day by British airborne forces. The target for Operation Goodwood was the Bourguebus ridge above Caen. Standing in the way of the British was a defensive position laid out in considerable depth by the newly appointed German commander of the Caen sector, General of Panzer Troops, Heinrich Eberbach. The frontline was held by the remnants of the 16th Luftwaffe Field Division. Behind it were the remnants of the 21st Panzer Division, supported by 88mm Flak guns and Tiger tanks. In reserve on the Bourguebus ridge were the *Leibstandarte* and part of the *Hitlerjugend* Divisions, and these units were to go into action under the command of the notorious Josef "Sepp" Dietrich.

■ *Left:* The arrival of the *Leibstandarte Adolf Hitler* Panzer Division in mid-July 1944 bolstered the German defences around Caen.

■ *Above:* Heavy camouflage protected German armour in the run-up to Operation Goodwood. This is a Tiger I sited in an ambush position.

This would be the first main test of the *Leibstandarte*'s panzer crews and many of its panzergrenadiers, who had only arrived at the front a week or so earlier. It is estimated that only some 14,000 men of the division were committed to the Normandy battle, because nearly 6000 trained recruits and logistic personnel were left behind at depots in Belgium. After more than a month's continuous fighting the *Hitlerjugend* Division was having a long-awaited rest in reserve, except for a strong Kampfgruppe under Max Wünsche, which Hitler ordered to the coast at the Orne estuary to counter a spurious invasion threat. Therefore the initial brunt of the coming fighting would fall on the *Leibstandarte*'s Panzer Regiment under the command of Jochen Peiper, with 59 Panzer IVs and 46 Panthers. The division's assault-gun battalion had some 35 StuG IIIs ready for action and the 101st SS Battalion's 25 Tiger Is. The famous victor of Villers-Bocage, Michael Wittmann, was now in command of this unit.

In total, the Germans could scrape together some 4800 infantry, around 200 tanks and 50 assault guns. In addition to this unconvincing force, they had 36 75mm antitank guns, 72 88mm Flak, 194 field guns and 17 Nebelwerfer rocket launchers. Their ability to blunt Operation Goodwood was doubtful.

The Bourguebus ridge gave German commanders a superb view of Caen below, and meant it was almost impossible for Montgomery to conceal his build-up. Radio intercept units first alerted the Germans to the coming offensive and Dietrich famously put his ear to the ground to listen for the vibration caused by the movement of so many tanks towards the front, a trick picked up during the massive tank battles in Russia.

## British onslaught

The Allied artillery barrage began at 05:25 hours on 18 July, and 10 minutes later the RAF bombers appeared overhead and started to unload their deadly cargo on the positions of the 21st Panzer and 16th Luftwaffe Divisions. After nearly 1000 Lancasters had passed over the target zones southeast of Caen, two further waves of bombers, mainly US B-17s, added to the carnage. Hundreds of Germans were killed or wounded, and much equipment damaged or destroyed. Massive 58.9-tonne (58-ton) Tiger tanks were turned upside down, and some German soldiers were driven insane by terror, but Montgomery's expectations for the bombardment soon proved to be very inaccurate. When the contrails of the last bombers disappeared just before 09:00 hours, the dazed defenders emerged from their bunkers, trenches, or under their tanks to man their defences. While the Luftwaffe division was devastated by the air attack and did not offer serious resistance, the German reserve positions were not so badly hit. All around the battlefield, small groups of determined Germans were preparing for what would happen next. The men of the Waffen-SS units were virtually untouched, and Dietrich immediately alerted them to be ready to counterattack the expected British onslaught.

■ *Below:* The Pak 43, the specialist antitank version of the famous 88mm Flak gun, was available in Normandy in large numbers. It could knock out any Allied tank then in service.

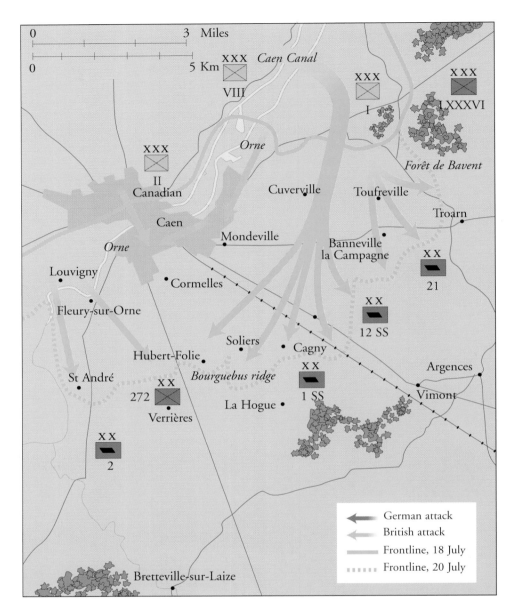

**■ Right:** The first phase of Operation Goodwood.

Moving forward first was the British 11th Armoured Division, with some 214 tanks of the 29th Armoured Brigade leading the way. These were arrayed in attack formation. The division's lead tank brigades moved out of the Orne bridgehead east of Caen with relative ease, covered by a rolling artillery barrage, then turned south before heading for Bourguebus ridge. In their wake there was chaos. There were not enough bridges for the follow-up artillery and supply units to cross the Orne River, and the 11th Armoured Infantry Brigade became bogged down in clearing two insignificant villages of a few isolated German defenders. When the Guards Armoured Division did get into action, instead of being able to move forward to help its sister division, it ran into just five 88mm Flak guns, eight infantrymen and six Tigers defending the village of Cagny and found itself bogged down for the rest of the day. One of the 29th Brigade's tank regiments was also sucked into this battle. The 7th Armoured Division was immobilized for the remainder of the day, not because of enemy gunfire, but because ahead of it were thick traffic jams which blocked the Orne River crossings.

Despite having taken a few hits from the 88mm Flak guns and Tigers in Cagny, the 29th Brigade continued to press on to its objective.

The remnants of the 21st Panzer's assault gun battalion had already started to engage the 29th Brigade's lead regiment, the Fife and Forfar Yeomanry, destroying more than 20 Shermans. It was to conduct a fighting withdrawal towards the *Leibstandarte*'s "stop line" on Bourguebus ridge. By 10:00 hours Wittmann's Tigers had already moved up and were ripping into the Shermans of the 3rd Royal Tank Regiment (3 RTR).

The *Leibstandarte*'s commander, SS-Brigadeführer Teddy Wisch, forward on the ridge, was engaged in conducting a detailed reconnaissance. For once, the Allied fighter-bombers were unsuccessful in stopping the movement of the German panzers, and by noon Peiper's Panther battalion was lying in wait. It had moved up into hull-down ambush positions on the northern slopes of the Bourguebus ridge, where a series of sunken roads provided superb cover for the Waffen-SS tanks. While the Panthers held the British advance, Wisch intended to use his assault gun battalion in order to hit the British armoured phalanx in the flank. Then the panzer regiment would be able to advance forward.

## Mobile battle

Peiper's Panthers fought a mobile battle. While his Panzer IVs and Tigers held ground, he led the Panthers forward four times on raids into the British tanks before withdrawing to cover in order to rearm and reorganize. At 12:45 hours the Panthers moved forward to the village of Soliers to engage the 29th Brigade for the first time. In the space of a few minutes, the Fife and Forfar Yeomanry lost 29 tanks. The regiment ceased to exist as a fighting formation. It took two hours for the British command to form a rescue column from the 23rd

■ *Below:* Cromwell tanks of the 7th Armoured Division were sent into battle alongside the 11th and Guards Armoured Divisions during Operation Goodwood.

Hussars, who had been bogged down fighting the 88mm Flak guns in Cagny. When they arrived below Bourguebus ridge they were greeted by the sight of dozens of Shermans burning across the hillside. Barely had the Hussars realized that there was no regiment to rescue from its predicament than they started to take hits from the combined force of *Leibstandarte*'s Panthers, Wittmann's Tigers and the 21st Panzer's StuG IIIs. Four tanks exploded within minutes of entering the battle, and soon another 16 were out action.

At this point the *Leibstandarte*'s StuG IIIs started to arrive, and Wisch fed them northwards to hit the right flank of 3 RTR. A further 20 British tanks were destroyed and the 29th Brigade began to waver; however, it did rally for just long enough to enable the Northamptonshire Yeomanry to attempt another move forward. But all of this was to no avail, and when 16 of its Cromwell tanks were knocked out, the regiment couldn't help but lose heart.

By nightfall panzer crews of the *Leibstandarte* were looking out on a tank graveyard. At least 160 of the 29th Brigade's 200 tanks were smouldering hulks. The Fife and Forfars and 3 RTR had each lost more than 40 tanks, while the Guards Armoured Division lost more than 60 tanks in its futile engagement with the 21st Panzer Division around Cagny.

The British claimed to have destroyed more than a dozen Panthers, but the day undoubtedly belong to Peiper's panzer crews. The lack of German infantry support meant Wisch was unable to press forward and mop up the hundreds of British tanks crews which were wandering around in front of his division's position among their destroyed vehicles. They received replacement tanks during the night, and the British were ready to attack again on 19 July.

> *By nightfall, the panzer crews of the* Leibstandarte *were looking out on a tank graveyard*

During the night the British desperately tried to sort out the dreadful traffic jams in the Orne bridgehead and reorganize their battered armoured divisions for another attack, this time with three divisions attacking abreast. Just after first light, 3 RTR tried to push forward against the *Leibstandarte*'s Panthers, only to run into a wall of fire. Pinned down, the regiment lost 43 of its 60 tanks and the remaining Shermans pulled back behind a railway embankment for safety. A rare intervention by Luftwaffe Messerschmitt fighters on a strafing run served further to undermine the morale of the British tank crews.

It would not be until late morning that General O'Connor, still commanding VIII Corps, managed to issue his orders to his shell-shocked and battered divisions for his coordinated attack. The attack could not be started until late afternoon, which gave Dietrich time to feed in the first elements of the *Hitlerjugend* Division, with two panzergrenadier battalions and some tanks, in between the right flank of the *Leibstandarte* and 21st Panzer. Wisch's remaining Panzer IVs were also brought into the "stop line" on Bourguebus ridge, and at last panzergrenadiers arrived in strength to give the *Leibstandarte*'s defensive line some depth. The British delay even allowed the

■ **Right:** Hundreds of RAF heavy bombers were sent to pummel the German defences east of Caen.

■ **Below:** General Montgomery concentrated his armour on a very narrow front in the hope of creating a decisive breakthrough.

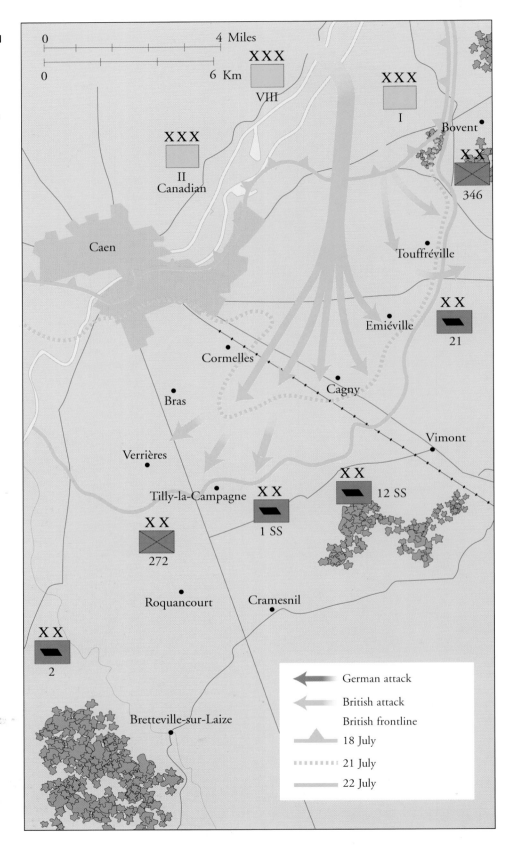

**Right:** The second phase of Operation Goodwood. As German resistance intensified, only marginal gains were made by the British and Canadians.

0    4 Miles
0    6 Km

XXX
VIII

XXX
I

XXX
II
Canadian

Bovent

XX
346

Caen

Touffréville

Emiéville

XX
21

Cormelles

Cagny

Bras

Vimont

Verrières

XX
12 SS

Tilly-la-Campagne

XX
1 SS

XX
272

Roquancourt

Cramesnil

XX
2

Bretteville-sur-Laize

German attack
British attack
British frontline
18 July
21 July
22 July

*Leibstandarte* to launch a limited counter-attack. Later on that same afternoon, Kampfgruppe *Wünsche* also returned to the front. It had been caught up in an anti-invasion wild-goose chase, but now it was back it was tasked with providing the beleaguered Dietrich with another armoured reserve. The anticipation for the coming battle was heightened no less by the fact that in many senses this would be the first time the two sister divisions of I SS Panzer Corps had fought side-by-side in battle.

> ## This would be the first time the sister divisions of I SS Panzer Corps had fought side-by-side in battle

### Taking on the Waffen-SS

Lined up from west to east to take on the Waffen-SS was the battered 11th Armoured Division and the fresh 7th Armoured Division, while the Guards Armoured Division was tasked with taking on the *Hitlerjugend*. Wisch favoured the tactic of concentrating most of his tanks in the centre of the line on the Desert Rats' axis of advance. This decision would leave the left flank of the division held only by panzer-grenadiers and a handful of StuG IIIs and 88mm Flak guns.

When the 11th Armoured began its attack at 16:00 hours, the German defence initially held. This was partly due to a map-reading error on the British side that sent the Northamptonshire Yeomanry driving across the front of the *Leibstandarte*'s line. It lost five tanks immediately. However, the now re-equipped 3 RTR pressed home the attack, and when it destroyed one of the two StuG IIIs holding the village of Bras, the other StuG withdrew. This was disastrous for the panzergrenadier battalion positioned in the village, as it now found itself without antitank protection. By 17:10 hours, 3 RTR and a British infantry battalion were mopping up in the village, and by the time they had finished, their total number of Waffen-SS prisoners stood at 300.

■ *Below:* British infantry played a minor role in the Goodwood battle, and their absence from the first wave of the assault meant a handful of German antitank guns were able to delay Montgomery's advance for a few crucial hours.

The Northamptonshire Yeomanry was now launched forward again to exploit this success, only to run into Peiper's Panthers and more StuG IIIS in hull-down firing positions. In the space of a few minutes, 32 Shermans were ablaze and the British regiment ceased to exist as a fighting unit. As his tanks were dealing with this attack, the weight of the 7th Armoured hit Peiper's main "stop line" in the centre of the Bourguebus ridge. The rapid loss of eight Shermans stopped the Desert Rats in their tracks, and they made no attempt to close with the *Leibstandarte*'s hull-down tanks and 88mm Flak guns.

Out on the *Leibstandarte*'s right flank, the *Hitlerjugend* found itself on the receiving end of the Guards Armoured's onslaught. Its defence was stiffened by the arrival of the first Panzerjäger IV self-propelled antitank guns, which boasted powerful L70 long-barrelled 75mm cannons. When the British attacked in the evening, the new weapons proved very effective, destroying several tanks and enabling the *Hitlerjugend* to hold its ground. The British even mistakenly identified the new Panzerjägers as feared 88mm Flak guns. The Guards did not press forward their attack in the face of the *Hitlerjugend*'s strong antitank screen, because waterlogged ground meant their tanks could not manoeuvre. The day of 19 July had been a major defensive success for I SS Panzer Corps, and during that day it had knocked out 65 of the 11th Armoured's tanks and scores of others along its front.

## The Canadians join the fray

The 7th Armoured Division tried its luck again against Peiper's tanks during the morning of 20 July and fared little better, with the County of London Yeomanry losing dozens more tanks to Panthers and Tigers. In the afternoon it was the turn of the Canadians to join Operation Goodwood from their bridgehead in southern Caen. With heavy

■ *Left:* When the British infantry finally got into action, it was too late to change the course of the battle.

■ *Below:* After receiving a heavy drubbing on the first day of Goodwood, Montgomery reorganized his armoured divisions and pressed forward again on 19 July.

fighter-bomber support, the Canadian 3rd Division hit the *Leibstandarte* panzergrenadiers and reconnaissance troops holding the division's extreme left flank. Typhoons weaved over the battlefield, strafing German tanks and gun positions with impunity. At first the air support proved decisive, and they drove back the Waffen-SS men from several villages. Then, at around 17:00 hours, a massive thunderstorm broke over the battlefield, at a stroke denying the Canadians their advantage. A *Leibstandarte* panzergrenadier battalion, backed by a company of StuG IIIs, was launched on a counterattack. The Saskatchewan Regiment was overrun and 208 men killed or captured. Then the Kampfgruppe moved against the Essex Scottish Regiment, sending it back in considerable disorder. *Leibstandarte* panzergrenadiers fought on through the night, pushing the Canadians back, to restore the German line, despite the almost constant heavy rain.

By dawn on 21 July, I SS Panzer Corps was holding firm. After the night's rain had engulfed the battlefield and turned it into a quagmire, Montgomery reluctantly called off the battle on the morning of 21 July. Operation Goodwood had spectacularly failed to achieve its stated objective: to capture the Bourguebus ridge and break open the German front east of Caen. Meanwhile, Montgomery had lost a total of 413 tanks and 6100 casualties in his futile offensive. Later, he claimed the offensive was only aimed at "writing down" or "attriting" the German panzer reserves and that more than 100 enemy tanks had been destroyed. In fact, less than 75 panzers and assault guns were hit during Operation Goodwood, and most of them were later repaired.

> *A massive thunderstorm broke over the battlefield, at a stroke denying the Canadians their advantage*

### Victory, at a price

Montgomery is on stronger ground when he claims his offensive had strategic implications because it diverted German armoured reserves from the west of the Normandy Front, allowing the US Army to break through at St Lô on 18 July. The famous British general was, however, perhaps using hindsight in claiming that this was his only intended objective for Operation Goodwood. The British had paid a high price for the slender strip of land captured

■ *Left:* Three days into Operation Goodwood, more than 400 British tanks were burning in the fields to the southeast of Caen.

and the modest losses inflicted. British and Canadian morale began to fall.

Montgomery did not give up his ambitions to destroy the German defenders southwest of Caen. The British general now planned a rolling series of offensives to keep Hausser and Bittrich's Waffen-SS panzer reserves occupied while the Americans launched their long-awaited decisive attack in the West.

The first of these offensives fell to the Canadians to conduct, and it would see them attacking the *Leibstandarte* on the Bourguebus ridge. They would be sent into attack over almost the same ground that O'Connor's VIII Corps had been butchered on six days before.

Operation Spring started with a night attack early in the morning of 25 July, after an air strike by 60 medium bombers. Then the Canadian infantry regiment of the 3rd Canadian Division advanced straight into the guns of the *Leibstandarte*. At 400m (437yd) in front of their lines, the Waffen-SS tanks and panzergrenadiers opened fire. The

North Nova Scotias were pinned down for more than 16 hours. Its supporting tank squadron was massacred by the *Leibstandarte*'s hull-down Panthers, losing 11 out of its 16 tanks. By the time the regiment pulled back under cover of dusk, only 100 men returned. The 3rd Division's attacked was stopped dead.

The 2nd Canadian Division simultaneously attacked the left flank of the *Leibstandarte*. They benefitted from the presence of a 17-pounder antitank gun battery that neutralized the Waffen-SS panzers and StuG IIIs, knocking out four tanks. Without panzer support, the *Leibstandarte* panzergrenadiers had to pull back, and by dawn the Royal Highland Light Infantry (RHLI) had captured the village of Verrières. British tanks of the 1st Royal Tank Regiment (1 RTR) were now sent forward to exploit this success. They ran into dug-in *Leibstandarte* StuG IIIs and soon British tanks were burning across the hillside. Later in the morning, it was the turn of the Black Watch of Canada to attack. They were

■ *Above:* German Nebelwerfer rocket batteries added to the havoc among Montgomery's assault troops, delaying his infantry at a key point in the battle.

■ *Above:* Tiger Is of the 101st SS Heavy Panzer Battalion were at the forefront of the German defence during Goodwood, hitting British Shermans at long ranges. This one was a victim of the battle.

enfiladed by panzer fire from high ground to the west, and their supporting tanks were decimated, so by the time they reached the crest of the Bourguebus ridge there only 60 men left. More than 300 dead and wounded were littering the battlefield by 17:00 hours.

Now the *Leibstandarte* launched a panzergrenadier counterattack, led by 10 Panzer IVs. They were closing in on the RHLI in Verrières when two squadrons of RAF Typhoons swooped down, rocketing three German tanks.

### Few gains for the Allies

When the full casualty returns started to arrive at II Canadian Corps' headquarters during the evening, senior commanders were horrified. More than 450 men were dead and some 1000 wounded, yet the frontline had only moved a few hundred metres farther south.

It took the British and Canadians six days to recover from the shock of Operation Spring. The 2nd Canadian Division was ordered to seize part of the summit of the Bourguebus ridge centred around Tilly-la-

Campagne. After initial skirmishing on the night of 29/30 July, the main attack went in at 02:30 hours on 31 July led by the Calgary Highlanders. All day long, vicious fighting raged through the village. Canadian tanks and RAF Typhoons were thrown into the battle but by the evening the *Leibstandarte* panzergrenadiers held firm. More than 200 Canadians were killed or wounded. For the next three days, the Canadians resorted to pounding the village with artillery and air strikes, in between daily attempts to storm it. Each time, they were driven off with heavy losses. For the *Leibstandarte* men holding out in the ruins of Tilly-la-Campagne, this period entered their division's folklore as the most intense bombardment it had endured in six years of war.

As the *Leibstandarte* held firm south of Caen, the *Hitlerjugend* was withdrawn from the front to act as reserve for Dietrich's I SS Panzer Corps. Almost two months into the Normandy campaign, Kurt Meyer's division had suffered 3500 casualties. Its operational tank strength stood at 61 Panthers, 39 Panzer IVs and 27 Panzerjäger IVs on 30

July, as well as 19 Tigers of the attached 101st SS Battalion. The *Leibstandarte* was in better shape, and had 61 Panzer IVs, 40 Panthers and 23 StuG IIIs ready for action.

## Operation Express

To the east of Dietrich's corps, Bittrich's *Frundsberg* Division had been holding firm on Hill 112 for more than two weeks, after the 43rd Division's failed attempt to take the strategic high ground. Montgomery kept feeding in units to keep up the pressure on the *Frundsberg* and 272nd Infantry Divisions. Thanks to the presence of the Tigers of the 102nd SS Battalion, most of these attempts failed with heavy losses. One Tiger was always kept on the hill's summit while the rest of the battalion's 19 tanks were held in reserve. Operation Express on 22 July saw two battalions of the Wiltshire Regiment,

*The Tigers and Churchills clashed head on; the British tanks were getting the worst of the engagement*

backed by the Churchills of the 9th Royal Tank Regiment (9 RTR), try to sweep up the eastern slope of the hill after they had taken the village of Maltot. The Tigers and Churchills clashed head on and the British tanks were getting the worst of the engagement, losing six tanks, when a forward air controller called down a squadron of Typhoons. The Tigers withdrew into cover, leaving the village in British hands along with 400 Wehrmacht prisoners. Hill 112 remained firmly in German hands for yet another week.

The *Hohenstaufen* Division was called back from the left flank of *Frundsberg* at the height of the Operation Goodwood battle and positioned in the Orne valley, guarding the southern suburbs of Caen. It helped the *Leibstandarte* defeat Montgomery's armoured offensive, forming a Kampfgruppe

■ *Left:* Attacks by Canadian infantry in the aftermath of Goodwood were repulsed by I SS Panzer Corps with heavy losses.

to take back three villages taken by Canadian troops. Early in the morning on 22 July, two of the division's Panthers led forward a panzergrenadier battalion which ran into heavy antitank gunfire. By the end of the day, 9 of the division's 24 Panthers were out of action, but the key villages were secured. As Operation Spring got underway against the *Leibstandarte* on 25 July, the *Hohenstaufen* was also hit hard by Canadian troops. To restore the line, the division's panzer regiment and 102nd SS Battalion Tigers rolled forward, inflicting heavy losses on the attacking tanks.

**French villagers came out to greet their liberators with long-hidden bottles of champagne**

Halted to the east, south and west of Caen by Hausser and Bittrich's panzer corps, Montgomery now switched the focus of his attack to the far west of the British sector. On 30 July, he launched Operation Bluecoat southwards towards Vire and Mount Pincon, with the 7th, 11th and Guards Armoured Divisions in the lead. II SS Panzer Corps was now diverted to block this move that punched a hole in the thinly held sector of the German line. *Hohenstaufen* led the move with 22 Panzer IVs, 29 Panthers and 27 StuG IIIs. The 102nd SS Battalion's 30 Tigers followed close behind. A "fast group" Kampfgruppe from *Hitlerjugend*, made up of a company of 13 Panthers and panzergrenadiers in armoured halftracks, was also sent to help Bittrich's corps. RAF Typhoons soon located the Waffen-SS tank columns in the afternoon on 2 August. They launched 923 sorties, destroying 13 tanks and 76 trucks, holding up the deployment of the Germans tanks for most of the day. British armour was advancing through open countryside and French villagers came out to greet their liberators with some long-hidden bottles of champagne.

The advance *Hohenstaufen* panzer Kampfgruppe engaged the 11th Armoured Division near le Beny-Bocage on the afternoon of 2 August, knocking out five Cromwells in the process. The Tigers went into action against the 23rd Hussars near

Chenedolle, turning a squadron's worth of Shermans into burning pyres. The bulk of I SS Panzer Corps was committed the following day and the British attack was brought to a standstill.

The 102nd SS Battalion's Tigers were in the forefront of the action around Vire, and conducted an ambush against the regimental headquarters of the Northamptonshire Yeomanry. Then *Frundsberg*'s panzer Kampfgruppe – with 7 Panzer IVs and 18 Panthers – entered the fray and were responsible for destroying 20 British tanks. This and other attacks carried out by the Waffen-SS panzers brought British tank losses since the start of Operation Bluecoat to a massive 200 vehicles.

Then Bittrich launched a counterattack into the rear of the British incursion at Chenedolle. *Hohenstaufen*'s Panthers were to account for 39 British tanks as they rolled forward, and they cut British supply lines. Panzergrenadiers stalked British tanks in the woods during the night, knocking out scores with Panzerfaust bazookas. Bittrich's tired troops kept pressing forward until the battle reached a climax on 6 August.

Bittrich had brought Operation Bluecoat to a halt, but his thinly stretched and tired troops could now do no more. They established a strong defensive line around Vire and made sure the British paid a heavy price if they tried to advance again. Over the following two days, Waffen-SS Tigers alone accounted for 38 British tanks.

Despite Bittrich's success, the foundations of the German front in Normandy were now starting to crack. Having received no reinforcements since late June, Waffen-SS officers were beginning to wonder whether they could hold on against the enemy for much longer.

■ *Below:* **Immediately after Goodwood, Montgomery began reorganizing his forces for yet another onslaught against the German line south of Caen.**

# CHAPTER 9

# DEATH OR GLORY

## Operation Cobra and the failure of Hausser's Mortain attack.

As Montgomery's armoured divisions were feeling the power of I SS Panzer Corps' Panthers and Tigers east of Caen, the US Army was in the process of launching an offensive that would eventually destroy the German armies in Normandy.

The fighting in the western half of Normandy was very different in nature from the open fields and villages around Caen. The constricted bocage terrain consisted of small fields lined by thick hedges and earthworks, as well as large areas of marshland that were impassable to tanks. It was a defender's paradise, so Rommel predominately deployed infantry divisions to contain the Americans.

A plethora of sunken roads, small woods and villages meant there was no room to manoeuvre large formations of tanks. The US Army quickly became bogged down in a series of small-scale engagements against dogged and expert German resistance. The so-called "Battle of the Hedgerows' would cost the Americans tens of thousands of casualties for little ground gained.

Like the British and Canadian armies in Normandy, the US Army contained a scattering of veterans from North Africa and Italy. Although the bulk of its troops in Normandy were well trained, they had no combat experience. During June and into July 1944, the German defenders of the Seventh Army under Paul Hausser managed to inflict a steady stream of casualties on the "green" US Army units sent against them. Hausser's veteran units, such as II Parachute Corps and the 352nd Infantry Division, made Lieutenant-General Omar Bradley's First US Army pay for every inch of terrain it captured. In

■ *Left: Das Reich* **Division Panthers tried in vain to hold back the US juggernaut in the western sector of the Normandy bridgehead.**

■ *Left:* St Lô was devastated by American firepower to free it from German rule.

a series of disjointed divisional offensives, the Americans suffered some 50,000 casualties and hardly dented the German front. The two US Army divisions that took the town of St Lô in mid-July lost a combined total of 5000 casualties in bitter, house-to-house fighting. One division lost an incredible 150 percent of its officers and 100 percent of its soldiers in six weeks of action. US divisions maintained their combat power by constant infusions of so-called "battlefield replacements", which did nothing for their unit cohesion, or the overall quality of their fighting expertise.

## Overwhelming firepower

It took the Americans a long time to master the terrain and their enemy. Their equipment, such as the Sherman tank, proved under-gunned and under-armoured compared to German Panthers and Tigers. One thing the Americans possessed in overwhelming quantities was firepower in the shape of heavy artillery and airpower. They unleashed it regularly against Hausser's troops and eventually the cunning Waffen-SS general was unable to compensate for the overwhelming material superiority enjoyed by the Americans. No matter how many GIs Hausser's troops killed, there always seemed to be two or three to take their place. By 24 July, the veteran *Panzer Lehr* Division, for example, could only put some 3000 men in the field and a few dozen tanks. Since the

**■ Right:** Operation Cobra and the American breakout from St Lô.

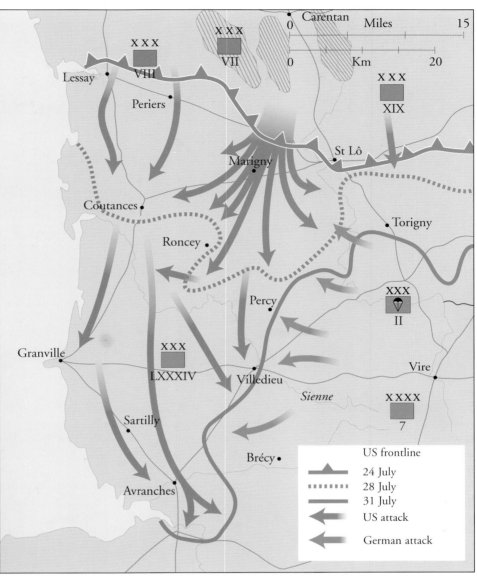

**■ Right:** Operation Cobra and the American breakout from St Lô.

**■ Below:** The US Army suffered horrendous losses trying to smash open the German line north of St Lô. Note the hedgerows that criss-crossed this area of France.

end of June only a trickle of German reinforcements had reached Normandy to replace the 100,000 casualties sustained by Rommel's armies in the month after D-Day. The German front was approaching breaking point, and Hausser was running out of reserves to plug the gaps.

The threat to Caen meant that the front facing the British attracted the bulk of Rommel's panzer reserves, and Hausser could not call on his beloved I or II SS Panzer Corps to help him in the West. In mid-June only one Waffen-SS division could be spared to counter the US Army's attempt to link its two bridgeheads, Omaha and Utah. Delayed by air attack, the 17th SS Panzergrenadier Division *Götz von Berlichingen* arrived at the Normandy front just as the US Army was about to link up its bridgeheads at Carentan. In a furious counterattack against the US 101st Airborne Division, led by the 42 StuG IIIs of its panzer battalion, the 17th SS Division lost some 450 casualties. The panzergrenadiers came to within 500m (547yd) of the town until a counterattack drove them back. The division then joined forces with the veteran 6th Parachute Regiment to block the advance of two US corps for nearly a month in vicious, close-quarter combat. Relations between the

■ *Above:* US
armour found it
almost impossible to
manoeuvre in the
Bocage terrain, until
special ploughs to
cut through the
hedgerows were
developed. Here, US
armour advances
during Operation
Cobra.

two units were strained at first, after Waffen-SS officers attempted to try the commander of the parachute unit for treason at a field court martial. His "crime" was that he had ordered a retreat.

To provide a panzer reserve for the German front facing the Americans, Rommel ordered the *Das Reich* Panzer Division to the Periers region. Its panzer regiment boasted almost 26 Panthers, 50 Panzer IVs and 36 StuG IIIs ready for action. It was in position in early July and was called forward into action on 3 July to counter a possible breakthrough by the US 30th Infantry and 3rd Armored Divisions. The terrain prevented the large-scale employment of tanks and the battle soon broke down into a series of small dogfights between individual German and American tanks. For two weeks the *Das Reich* troopers were locked in combat with the American GIs. Their greater battle experience and superior equipment meant they were more often than not able to get the better of the Americans, but in its first week of action, the division lost just

over 1200 men and some 30 tanks or assault guns, losses it could ill-afford.

## Breakout from Normandy

After a frustrating time fighting up the Cherbourg peninsular to capture the port city on 27 June, Bradley was able to turn his attention southwards during July, and began to plan for the breakout from Normandy. The idea was to open a breach and then drive southwards to Avranches, then Lieutenant-General George Patton's Third Army would carry on the advance, swinging westwards to eventually encircle and destroy the German forces.

Chastized by his experiences to date, Bradley was determined to concentrate American firepower in a narrow sector to overwhelm the defenders. A 7000m (7655yd) section of front to the west of St Lô was selected as the target for Lieutenant-General J. Lawton Collins' VII Corps in the appropriately named Operation Cobra. The plan called for 1500 heavy bombers, 380 medium bombers and 550 fighter-bombers to drop more than 4064 tonnes (4000 tons) of explosives on a target box that stretched 2500m (2734yd) behind the front. More than 1000 guns would join the barrage. Four fresh American divisions would then be unleashed. On paper, the plan looked unstoppable.

The offensive got off to an inauspicious start on 25 July when cloud obscured part of the target and part of the bomber force dropped its deadly cargo on US troops waiting to go into the attack, killing more than 100 and wounding almost 500. The effect on the *Panzer Lehr* Division, positioned in the centre of the target box, was even worse, though. Almost 1000 men died, and a regiment and a whole Kampfgruppe were put out of action, along with all the division's tanks and guns. Despite this onslaught, the survivors came out of their trenches and bunkers fighting, holding up the offensive for 48 hours. Then Bradley committed the 2nd "Hell on Wheels" Armored Division *en masse*. Unlike

*The bomber force dropped its deadly cargo on US troops, killing more than 100 and wounding 500*

Dietrich east of Caen, Hausser had no reserves to plug the breach in his line because Bradley had ordered all his troops to stage diversionary attacks to tie down German forces along the whole of the Normandy Front. Disaster threatened.

Hausser had tried to pull *Das Reich*'s Panther battalion out of the line to the west to throw against the American breakthrough, but it could not disengage in time. In the end only five Panthers made it to help the *Panzer Lehr*, and they were soon put out of action. The breakthrough broke the cohesion of the German front. By 27 July, huge columns led by 600 American tanks were streaming south towards Avranches with nothing to stop them. German units started to crack under the stain of constant American attacks and almost six weeks of fighting without relief. The *Das Reich* and 17th SS Divisions managed to pull back and form a line north of Coutances on 27 July, which held the Americans at bay for a day.

■ **Below:** Lieutenant-General J. Lawton Collins (centre) was one of the few US Army commanders fully to master the art of fighting in the Bocage.

Then the front behind them collapsed, and the two Waffen-SS divisions and the army's 353rd Infantry Division were soon trapped in a pocket south of Roncey. Fuel was running short and scores of tanks had to be abandoned. In the chaos, *Das Reich's* commander, SS-Brigadeführer Heinz Lammerding, was wounded and then his replacement, the division's panzer regiment commander, SS-Obersturmbannführer Christian Tychsen, was killed in action. On the night of 28/29 July, the trapped troops made a bid for freedom, cutting through the loose cordon of US troops around them. Dodging past most of the Americans, the column clashed with a US armoured regiment.

The American tanks came off worst in the encounter, and by dawn on 30 July the three units were free. In their wake they had left roads littered with abandoned tanks, trucks, guns and other debris of war. US troops rounded up 4000 prisoners in the aftermath of the German escape bid. By the end of the month, some 20,000 Germans would be in American prison camps and Patton's tanks would be in Avranches.

## The madness of Operation Luttich

In his headquarters in East Prussia, Hitler at first forbade any retreat in the face of the American onslaught. Then the Führer demanded a counterattack. Looking at the map table in Rastenburg, the solution looked simple. Eight of the nine panzer divisions in Normandy were to strike into the flank of the American incursion to cut off Patton's tanks.

To the likes of Hausser and the commanders of the divisions given the dubious honour of participating in Operation Luttich, the whole thing was total madness. All their units were seriously understrength, short of ammunition and fuel. For example, most of the panzer units would be disengaged from the Caen Front, where Montgomery's troops were also strongly pressing forward. Then they were expected to move almost 100km (62 miles) under constant Allied air attack to their concentration area, before massing for the assault. One veteran army divisional commander refused to participate in this crazy enterprise, and was sacked for his efforts.

The aftermath of the 20 July Bomb Plot against Hitler was still being felt in the ranks of the German forces in Normandy. When scores of army officers in France were arrested and executed for their part in the plot, rumours spread that they had been sabotaging the war effort. Mistrust grew between ardent Nazis and anyone who did not seem to show the necessary level of enthusiasm for continuing the struggle. So when senior officers, including Waffen-SS veterans such as Hausser, Dietrich and Bittrich, heard of the Führer's attack plans they were dismayed, but had to be careful about public criticism of it. They went along with it because there was no alternative. Disobedience of the Führer was not an option at this time. Hitler was determined that the attack would go ahead, and he even took the planning out of the hands of his now mistrusted field commanders. A senior officer was dispatched from the Führer's headquarters with the

■ *Above:* As commander of the German Seventh Army, Paul Hausser fought a masterful delaying action in the west of Normandy in the face of overwhelming odds.

■ *Left:* German infantry were the backbone of the Wehrmacht defence in the West, but they suffered grievously in the face of massive American firepower.

detailed plan for Operation Luttich, even down to routes of march and artillery fire plans. Hausser and his commanders were given little choice in the matter. It was a case of take it, or leave it.

Not surprisingly morale among the attackers, even in the ranks of the once ultra-loyal Waffen-SS, was at rock bottom. Operation Luttich was viewed as a total suicide mission.

The balance of forces looked terrible. In total the Germans could muster only 750 operational tanks left in Normandy at the end of July, out of a total of 2200 sent to the front during June and July. The combined British and American armies had landed more than 6000 tanks in France since D-Day.

General of Panzer Troops Hans von Funck's XLVII Panzer Corps' headquarters was given command of the attack, which Hitler said was only to begin when all the eight panzer divisions were in place. By 6

> *The Germans could muster only 750 tanks left in Normandy, out of a total of 2200 sent to the front*

August the size of the American breach was getting totally out of control. Thousands of American tanks and vehicles were pushing through Avranches. British tanks continued to push through their breach at Vire, tying down II SS Panzer Corps and preventing it from joining Operation Luttich. Even through he had only been able to gather together four of his expected eight panzer divisions, and hardly any of the promised Luftwaffe fighters were ready, Hausser decided it was now or never. He ordered Operation Luttich to go ahead on 7 August.

At hand were the 2nd, 116th and *Panzer Lehr* Divisions, as well as part of the *Leibstandarte* and *Das Reich*, which were reinforced with the remnants of the 17th SS Division. All told, Funck had a paltry 185 tanks to turn the tide of the war in Germany's favour.

Allied air supremacy was now such a problem for the Germans that Hausser ordered the attack to begin under the cover of darkness at 02:00 hours on 7 August. Surprise was to be of the essence; accordingly, there was no preparatory bombardment. Hitler's micro-management of the planning for the attack meant all the key documents had been delivered by hand to the German commanders in France. This had the unintentional spin-off of ensuring that the British ULTRA code-breaking operation was not able to pick up any German radio traffic about the impending attack. Unaware of the coming onslaught, Bradley had only stationed the tired and understrength US 30th Infantry Division to guard the town of Mortain, which was the first objective of Operation Luttich. It had no warning of the impending attack.

Waffen-SS participation in the Mortain counterattack, as Operation Luttich is now known, centred around three main units. SS-Standartenführer Otto Baum commanded a Kampfgruppe made up from the *Das Reich* and 17th SS Divisions. Its objective was Mortain itself. The *Leibstandarte* was thrown into the battle piecemeal because of delays in moving the division from the Caen Front along congested roads and under incessant Allied air attack. Only a single panzer battalion with 43 Panthers and seven Panzer IVs, along with the *Leibstandarte*'s reconnaissance unit and an armoured halftrack-mounted panzergrenadier battalion, arrived in time to go with the first attack wave. The rest of the division was several hours' march behind.

■ *Below:* Once they had broken through at St Lô, the Americans began to round up tens of thousands of German prisoners.

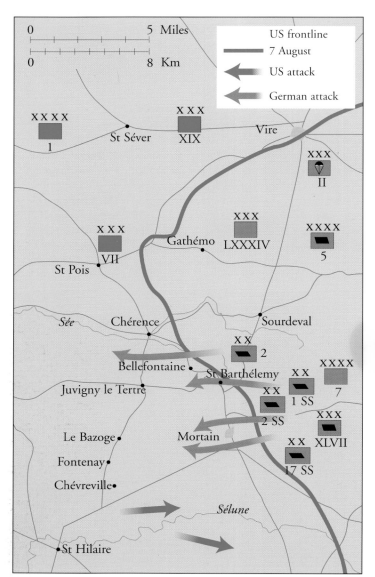

**Above: The ill-fated German Mortain counterattack.**

317 on the eastern edge of the town. To the west of Mortain, the US 120th Infantry Regiment fought desperate rearguard actions, which they hoped would buy time until daylight and the arrival of air support.

## Surprise at le Mesnil-Tôve

North of Mortain, the advance units of the *Leibstandarte* were assigned to the 2nd Panzer Division. SS-Sturmbannführer Gustav Knittel's reconnaissance troops raced ahead of the tank force, spreading confusion in the American ranks. They surprised a US column near le Mesnil-Tôve and captured a large quantity of trucks and antitank guns, before pressing on a further 3km (1.8 miles) faced by little opposition. By late morning, however, strong American road-blocks were in place and Knittel's men had to pull back to defend le Mesnil-Tôve.

Just before dawn, the *Leibstandarte*'s tanks and panzergrenadier battalion began their attack on the strongly held village of St Barthélemy, after a 45-minute artillery barrage. While 30 Panzer IVs and infantry of the 2nd Panzer were tasked with taking the northern half of the village, the *Leibstandarte* was to take the southern section.

Heavy fog hung over the battlefield, making it impossible for the German tanks to engage the defenders in the village at long range, so a combined tank-infantry assault was ordered to storm the American positions. By 11:30 hours the German tanks were on the far side of the village, but small groups of Americans were still holding out in cellars and bunkers. It was early afternoon before the Germans had cleared the village, and they captured almost 400 Americans in the process. The delay gave Bradley time to regroup and bring up reserves to contain the German attack. The US general still needed another day before he could be in a position to counterattack, so he turned to the Allied air forces to contain the German tank columns. By early afternoon the fog that had covered the Mortain region was finally lifting, at last exposing Funck's troops to devastating aerial attack.

Just after 12:15 hours on 7 August, the first of 271 RAF Typhoon fighters took off from forward airstrips in Normandy, their target the huge German tank and vehicle

At first the German attack went well. *Das Reich* stormed into Mortain, scattering surprised American units out of its path. Its panzer regiment pushed past the town and headed 5km (3.1 miles) westwards. The division's reconnaissance battalion secured its left flank, moving 4km (2.5 miles) south of the town, which was soon the scene of fierce fighting between American infantry and Waffen-SS panzergrenadiers. The 17th SS Division's reconnaissance battalion hit the town from the front and *Das Reich*'s *Der Führer* Panzergrenadier Regiment swept in from the north. A battalion of American infantry were surrounded on the crucial Hill

columns around Mortain. The Luftwaffe was nowhere to be seen. It took the RAF fighters 45 minutes to appear over the battlefield and they started to circle, looking for targets. For the next nine hours, the RAF squadrons maintained a constant presence over the battlefield. At any one time, there were never less than 22 aircraft overhead.

## Swooping Typhoons

The German attack stalled as the Typhoons swooped to rocket and machine-gun any tanks or trucks they could find. Waffen-SS men dived for shelter and tried to drive their vehicles under cover, but it was to no avail. All afternoon the German columns were relentlessly attacked from the air. There was no prospect of any kind of advance. Columns of *Leibstandarte* tanks and trucks heading towards the battlefield were also caught in the air onslaught, further blunting the momentum of the German attack. One column was held up for several hours when an Allied fighter crashed on the lead German tank, blocking the road ahead. The RAF pilots claimed 84 tanks destroyed, 35 probably destroyed and 21 damaged, with another 112 vehicles hit. This was perhaps an exaggeration, but when the Germans pulled out of the sector a few days later, they left behind 43 Panthers, 10 Panzer IVs, 23 armoured halftracks, 8 armoured cars and 46 other vehicles. This was the first time ever in the history of warfare that airpower by itself had halted a ground force.

As darkness fell, the Germans tried to reorganize their battered forces and bring up more reserves. The continued resistance of the trapped Americans on Hill 317 outside Mortain thwarted *Das Reich*'s attempt to advance forward throughout the night and the following day.

More fog in the morning of 8 August provided the reinforced *Leibstandarte* with the opportunity to move forward towards Juvigny and Bellefontaine in strength. Now Bradley's reserves were in place and the *Leibstandarte*'s panzers ran into sustained antitank gunfire and were stopped in their tracks. American tanks went on the offensive against the 2nd Panzer, forcing Knittel's depleted reconnaissance troops out of le Mesnil-Tôve by the evening.

Not all the *Leibstandarte* Division was able to get through to join the attack, and a strong Kampfgruppe had to be diverted northwards to seal an American incursion south of Vire which threatened the right flank of the attacking units.

American air and artillery fire now began to rain down on the German units around Mortain, again stalling any idea of pressing home the attack towards Avranches. It was no longer a case of pushing forwards, but holding out against overwhelming odds. Throughout 9 and 10 August, increasing numbers of American tanks were pressing forward against the Waffen-SS lines. The German Panthers destroyed many Shermans in this unequal struggle.

Just as it was becoming clear that Operation Luttich was running out of steam,

■ *Below:* Acts of amazing bravery by individual Waffen-SS officers, such as *Das Reich*'s tank ace Ernst Barkmann, were no longer enough to hold the line in Normandy.

Hitler insisted on ordering more units to reinforce the attack. II SS Panzer Corps was ordered to pull out of the line southwest of Caen, where it was fighting Montgomery's Operation Bluecoat to a halt, in spite of protests from its commander, Willi Bittrich, to be sent westwards to reinforce Funck's doomed enterprise. The *Frundsberg* Division eventually managed to break free from the front near Vire and moved into position on the left of *Das Reich* during the night of 7/8 August. Heavy air attacks prevented it attacking towards Berenton until the morning of 9 August, when a grand total of 12 panzers were launched forward and four were quickly knocked out. Further British tank attacks north of Vire meant that the *Hohenstaufen* Division had to remain there to contain this breakthrough and could not be sent to join the Mortain Offensive.

Hausser had ordered that all attempts to continue the attack on Avranches should stop on the afternoon of 11 August, and soon afterwards began preparing plans for a withdrawal to a more defensible line to the east. Now the Waffen-SS units were desperately short of fuel because of the incessant air attacks, and many tanks and other vehicles had to be abandoned. Two days later, the *Leibstandarte* reported having only 14 Panzer IVs, 7 Panthers and 8 StuG IIIs operational. *Das Reich* was in an even worse condition, with only five Panzer IVs, three Panthers and eight StuG IIIs in the line.

In his eastern Prussian bunker, the Führer was furious at the failure of the attack and wanted a scapegoat. He ordered Funck sacked on 11 August. The following day, US tanks broke through *Das Reich*'s lines and relieved the trapped GIs on Hill 317. Of the 700 who had been surrounded five days earlier, only 400 were still fit for action. The US Army, backed by RAF Typhoons, had taken on the élite of the Waffen-SS and stopped it

■ *Below:* British armour soon joined the attack in the west, making it impossible for the Germans to restore their defence line.

in its tracks. The contribution of airpower in stopping the Mortain attack should not be underestimated.

For the Mortain operation the Luftwaffe centralized its few fighter resources and attempted to intervene over the battlefield, but Allied air superiority ensured that German aircraft were shot down as soon as they took off, and not one Luftwaffe aircraft appeared over the battlefield. As mentioned above, the weather was at first poor, but as it improved Typhoons swarmed over the area. There were so many that some got in each other's way, and several midair collisions resulted. On the first day Typhoons flew a total of 294 sorties over the battlefield.

One notable incident was the battle between 245 Squadron and the 1st SS Panzer Division on the road near St Barthélemy. Their first attacks sprayed the tanks and transports with rocket and cannon fire, then

the Typhoons broke off as they exhausted their ammunition and rockets, returning again to their airstrip to refuel and rearm. So intensive were the sortie rates that 245 Squadron afterwards referred to 7 August as "The Day of the Typhoon".

German commanders were shocked at the magnitude of the Allied air attacks at Mortain, which would be repeated later around Falaise. Major-General Rudolf-Christoph Freiherr von Gersdorff, the chief of staff of the German Seventh Army, subsequently agreed that the continuation of the counterattack towards Avranches was a mistake. Contributing to the German failure was the overemphasis of attacking north, between Mortain and Vire, rather than farther south. The failure of the offensive set the stage for the next and even greater disaster to befall German arms in France: the Battle of the Falaise Pocket.

> *So intensive were the sorties that 245 Squadron referred to 7 August as "The Day of the Typhoon"*

■ *Above:* **With the road south open, Lieutenant-General George Patton's Third Army was unleashed. German defeat in Normandy was now assured.**

# CHAPTER 10

# DEATH OF THE HITLER YOUTH

## Operation Totalize and the defeat of 12th SS Panzer.

After blunting Operation Luttich, the Allied High Command saw that it had the opportunity to trap the German armies in Normandy in a giant pocket. General Patton's Third Army was fanning out virtually unopposed into Brittany and moving rapidly eastwards, heading towards the Seine River crossings. All that was needed was for the noose to be closed around the 400,000 Germans still fighting in Normandy. Montgomery decided that now was the time to blast through the German defences east of Caen, and push south to link up with Patton's spearhead. Operation Totalize was to begin on 8 August 1944.

Two infantry divisions, each led by an armoured brigade, were to advance due south along the main road out of Caen towards Falaise, on Route Nationale 158. This would be a very different style of attack to those previously attempted by the British or Canadians. Seven separate armoured columns would be formed, with as many

■ *Left:* A *Hitlerjugend* panzergrenadier examines the aftermath of yet another failed Allied attack south of Caen.

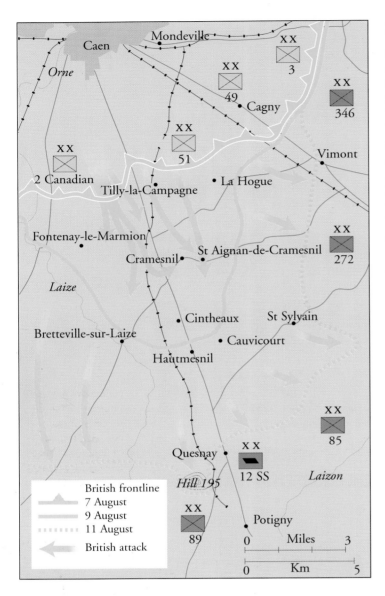

**Above: Operation Totalize ripped apart the German front south of Caen.**

infantry as possible loaded on armoured personnel carriers which had been created by converting self-propelled artillery pieces. For the first time, tanks would lead the way at night, guided by artificial moonlight from searchlight batteries. Mine-clearing "flail" tanks, armoured bulldozers and flame-thrower "Crocodile" tanks were at the front of each armoured column, leading 200 armoured vehicles. Huge air support was laid on as normal, but this time it was aimed not just at the German frontline positions, but also at reserve units and reinforcement routes. This Allied force also had one major advantage over previous units that had

attempted to seize the Bourguebus ridge. This time there were no Waffen-SS tanks and 88mm Flak guns waiting for them. The *Leibstandarte* had been pulled out to lead the attack on Mortain, II SS Panzer Corps was fighting Operation Bluecoat to a halt near Vire, and the *Hitlerjugend* was in reserve. "Sepp" Dietrich was still in command of the sector, although his I SS Panzer Corps headquarters had only one Waffen-SS division, *Hitlerjugend*, with 59 Panthers, 39 Panzer IVs, 27 Jagdpanzer IVs and the 8 Tigers of the 101st SS Battalion under its command. They faced more than 700 British, Canadian and Polish tanks.

At 23:00 hours on the evening of 7 August, 1020 RAF bombers began the preparatory bombardment. As the 3517 tonnes (3462 tons) of bombs were exploding, the armoured columns started their engines and moved forward into the attack. The bombing finished on time and the assault tanks were able to cross the start-line at exactly 23:00 hours.

## Meyer's stop line

For the next six hours, the columns pushed nearly 5km (3.1 miles) into the stunned German 89th Infantry Division. Resistance was patchy, but in terms of the previous attempts to take the Bourguebus ridge, the assault troops suffered relatively low casualties: in the region of 300 men spread evenly between seven battalion-sized units. As dawn was breaking, the Allied troops had for all intents and purposes blasted open the German front. Shell-shocked survivors were streaming away from the fighting. For a few hours only one man stood between the Allies and victory: the *Hitlerjugend*'s commander, Kurt Meyer.

He had rushed to the threatened sector to carry out a reconnaissance, and early in the morning stood on Route 158 as hordes of fleeing German infantry rushed past. Armed only with a carbine, he shamed the soldiers into standing firm with a couple of *Hitlerjugend* Panzerjäger IVs that had just arrived in the village of Cintheaux.

By midday, Meyer had brought up his battalion of Panzer IV's, some Panzerjäger IVs, and Michael Wittmann's Tigers to his improvised "stop line". Not content with just holding the attack, Meyer was going to attack. His mind was made up when he saw an American B-17 flying overhead dropping flares to mark targets for follow-up waves of bombers. The panzers would be safer from the American bombs if they mixed with the British, Canadian and Polish tanks. Wittmann's Tigers led the Panzerkeil (or wedge) forward. Meyer briefly climbed on to the Waffen-SS Tiger ace's tank to wish him luck, not knowing that this would be Wittmann's last battle.

Meyer's unconventional tactics paid off. The panzer charge escaped the B-17s and drove headlong into the Polish armoured regiment and the British 33rd Armoured Brigade. The terrain was open and the Allied tanks had little cover from the German 75mm and 88mm high-velocity cannons. Wittmann's Tigers swung off Route 158 and hit the Canadian 4th Armoured Division. It was stopped dead, losing scores of tanks, but two Tigers were knocked out. Undeterred, Wittmann pressed on eastwards against the flank of the British Northamptonshire Yeomanry, blasting another 20 Shermans as he went. Hopelessly outnumbered, Wittmann pressed on towards St Aignan-de-Cramesnil. British Sherman Firefly tanks,

*Meyer climbed on to Wittmann's tank to wish him luck, not knowing that this would be his last battle*

armed with the powerful 17-pounder gun-firing tungsten sabot rounds, were waiting in ambush for the Tigers. A Squadron of the Yeomanry is credited with putting an end to Wittmann's career which, to his credit, took in 138 tank kills. Five tanks zeroed in on Wittmann's Tiger, and consequently the turret was seen to explode after a sabot round succeeded in penetrating the tank's armour. There were no survivors.

More Panzer IVs now joined the battle from the south, intercepting the 1st Polish Armoured Division's lead regiment and putting 24 Shermans out of action. *Hitlerjugend* 88mm Flak guns were also in action against the Poles to great effect. Again, the intervention of the *Hitlerjugend* Division had thwarted the Allied plans. Scores of Shermans were burning and the Allied advance was brought to a halt. It cost Meyer 178 men, 5 Tigers and 6 Panzer IVs. Lacking the manpower to hold a continuous front during the night against such overwhelming odds, Meyer ordered his forward Kampfgruppe to fall back to a new line centred on the high ground around Point 140, 5km (3.1 miles) to the south, where the bulk of Max Wünsche's panzer regiment was now gathering.

■ *Below:* German antitank defences south of Caen included Pak 43 88mm guns. They inflicted a massive toll on British, Canadian and Polish armour.

■ *Right:* Field Marshal Hans von Kluge replaced Rundstedt as supreme German commander in the West, but he made little impact on the steadily deteriorating situation at the front.

destroyed on Point 140. It was not until nightfall that 49 Canadians were able to escape back to Polish lines. In contrast to these losses, not a single German panzer was lost in the course of the battle.

His battered troops held their lines for one more day, until Hitler ordered the division to be pulled out of the line to be sent westwards, to reinvigorate the now-stalled

In the confusion, the retreating German units became lost and this allowed the Canadian 28th Armoured Regiment and the Algonquin Infantry Battalion to slip through their lines to occupy Point 140. The result was a massacre. Wünsche's Panthers were to their front and five Tigers on high ground to the west. All day the Canadians were trapped on the exposed hillside, which had now become a "killing zone" raked by 88mm, 75mm, Nebelwerfer, mortar and machine-gun fire. Standing off outside the range of the Canadian Shermans, the Tigers and Panthers systematically wiped out all vehicles on the hillside. In desperation, the Canadians tried to call in RAF Typhoons to rocket the German tanks, only to have them attack their own tanks by mistake.

## The last great success

When Canadian units were sent to relieve the cut-off troops, Meyer's men ambushed them, knocking out 26 tanks and turning them back. In the afternoon the Poles tried to get through to them, only to run into a wall of Panzerjäger IVs, and they lost 22 Shermans. They got close enough to the trapped regiments to bring down fire support, but mistook the Canadian tanks for German ones and started firing on them. Some 125 men were killed and 47 tanks

Operation Luttich. In the three-day battle, the Canadians lost 80 tanks and the Poles admitted the destruction of 66 of their tanks. The battle had not been all one-sided, with Meyer losing 414 casualties. His tank strength was now reduced to 20 Panzer IVs and 15 Panthers. Thanks to the arrival of additional tanks from the 102nd SS Battalion, he now boasted 15 Tigers.

This was the last notable defensive success for the men of Meyer's division. The great Allied jaws were now closing around the German armies in Normandy, and it was becoming clear that these German armies were being pushed further and further towards the town of Falaise. It was apparent that in a matter of days, the struggle for supremacy in the northwest would be over.

■ *Below:* **Flamethrowers spearhead the Canadian advance during Operation Totalize.**

# CHAPTER 11

# FALAISE KESSEL

## The defeat of the German armies in Normandy.

**W**hile Kurt Meyer's panzer crews were duelling with Montgomery's tanks on the road out of Caen, the German front in Normandy was in the process of collapsing. Everywhere Allied spearheads were probing forward and meeting ever-weaker resistance. South of Caen the Canadians and Poles were pushing towards Falaise, facing the remnants of the Fifth Panzer Army, now under the command of "Sepp" Dietrich. In the centre of the Allied line, the British Second Army was continuing to follow up Willi Bittrich's II SS Panzer Corps through Vire. To the east of Mortain, the depleted German forces that had tried to break through to Avranches were staging a fighting retreat under the command of Paul Hausser's Seventh Army. Patton's Third Army was racing eastwards past Le Mans and on 8 August it turned northwards, aiming for Argentan. Five days later, American tanks were outside the town, barely 32km (20 miles) away from the Canadians at Falaise.

Hans von Kluge, the commander of Army Group B, was pleading with Hitler to allow a withdrawal of the 400,000 troops which were now threatened with encirclement. The Führer ordered Kluge to stand and fight. The German armies were now being pressed into an ever-smaller area between Falaise and Argentan, and relentlessly pounded with artillery and air strikes. Kluge drove to visit Dietrich's headquarters on 15 August, and got stuck in the maelstrom for several hours after his convoy was strafed by Allied fighters and his radio truck destroyed. Suspicious that Kluge had been trying to negotiate

■ *Left:* As the Normandy Front collapsed, an increasing number of Waffen-SS officers and soldiers entered Allied captivity.

■ **Above:** The men of the 17th SS Panzergrenadier Division *Götz von Berlichingen* were in the forefront of the final battles to hold the Falaise Pocket open.

a surrender with the Allies during the time he was out of radio contact, Hitler ordered him back to Berlin. Fearful of his fate once he was away from his headquarters, Kluge bit on a cyanide capsule and was dead in seconds. The next most senior general in Normandy was Hausser, so he was appointed to command all the troops trapped in the Falaise Kessel (or kettle). This was the German term for encircled troops and was apt. With every hour the Allies were increasing the pressure on the trapped troops until it was reaching boiling point.

No matter what orders Hitler issued from his East Prussian bunker, the commanders and troops on the ground in France were starting to take matters into their own hands. Kluge's replacement, Field Marshal Walther Model, reluctantly agreed to order a withdrawal on the 16th to set up a new line on the Dives River, but the senior Waffen-SS officers, who now held all the important commands in the Kessel, had been pulling back for five days. They had realized that the battle was lost and that every effort had to be made to get as many troops out of the Kessel as possible.

The *Leibstandarte*, *Das Reich* and 17th SS Divisions east of Mortain had been the

> *The commanders on the ground in France were beginning to take matters into their own hands*

first to fall back. Threatened by encirclement by American tanks to the south and British armour from the north, they staged a brief rearguard action on the Orne River at Putanges on the night of 17/18 August. After its sister divisions had safely crossed at midnight, the *Leibstandarte* blew up the last bridge and slipped away. II SS Panzer Corps was next to go, ordered to fall back through Argentan to form a counterattack force.

The *Hitlerjugend* was still holding off the Canadians and Poles on the northern shoulder of the Kessel. Behind it, chaos reigned, with huge truck convoys trying to move eastwards under relentless Allied air attack and causing massive traffic jams. The Waffen-SS divisions fared better than most, and the vast majority of their support elements managed to escape eastwards before the pocket was sealed on 20 August. Fuel shortages were beginning to bite, and an increasing number of tanks and other vehicles had to be abandoned when their tanks ran dry. Overhead, Allied aircraft were pounding the Germans: 37 P-47 Thunderbolt pilots of the 36th Group, for example, found 800 to 1000 enemy vehicles of all types milling about in the pocket west of Argentan. They could see American and British forces racing to close off the gap. They went to work. Within an hour the Thunderbolts had blown up or burned out between 400 and 500 enemy vehicles. The fighter-bombers kept at it until they ran out of bombs and ammunition. One pilot, with empty gun chambers and bomb shackles, dropped his belly tank on 12 trucks and left them all in flames. One Typhoon pilot recalled: "The show starts like a well-planned ballet: the Typhoons go into echelon while turning, then dive on their prey at full throttle. Rockets whistle, guns bark, engines roar and pilots sweat without noticing it as our missiles smash the Tigers. Petrol tanks explode amid torrents of black smoke. A Typhoon skids away to avoid machine-gun fire. Some horses frightened by the noise gallop wildly in a nearby field."

Typhoons typically would destroy the vehicles at the head of a road column, then shoot up the rest of them with their rockets and cannon. When they had finished, Spitfires would dive down to strafe the remains.

## Chaos in the Kessel

Elements of 23 German divisions were in the Kessel. Command and control was breaking down; the frontline was being held by only small determined groups of men formed into *ad hoc* Kampfgruppen. The Allied pincers were closing in and, late on 18 August, a corridor only a few kilometres wide remained open. Hitler now tried to pretend that a new front should be established on the Seine. All that the German commanders in the pocket were worried about was getting out alive.

Hausser ordered the II SS Panzer Corps and *Das Reich*, which were now outside the Kessel, to hold open a corridor for the remainder of the troops trapped inside. During the afternoon of 19 August, escape orders were issued at an impromptu conference in a quarry. Hausser, Meyer, Teddy Wisch of the *Leibstandarte* and the three senior army officers left in the Kessel worked out the plan.

The last remaining tanks were put at the head of columns and the breakout began. The now wounded Meyer himself led one column, riding in the turret of a Panzer IV, tank accompanied by his chief of staff, SS-Sturmbannführer Hubert Meyer. Eventually, the *Hitlerjugend* command group was forced to make their way on foot through the night until they reached German lines.

■ *Below:* US troops watch Allied airpower and artillery pound the trapped remnants of the German Army in the Falaise Pocket.

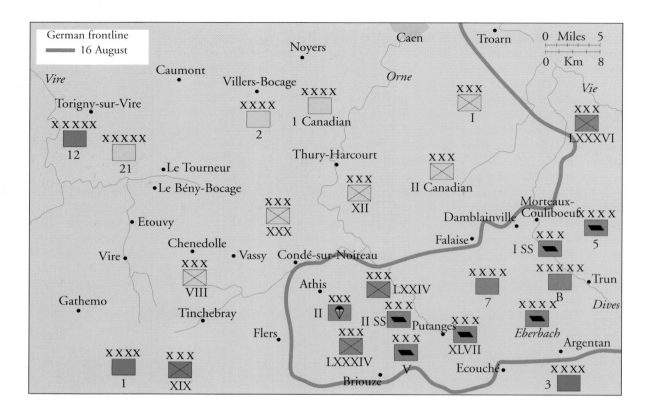

German frontline
16 August

Caen · Troarn · 0 Miles 5

Noyers · Orne · 0 Km 8

Caumont · Vie

Vire · Villers-Bocage · XXXX · 1 Canadian

XXXX · 2 · I

Torigny-sur-Vire · XXX · LXXXVI

XXXXX · 12 · XXXXX · 21

Le Tourneur · Thury-Harcourt · XXX · II Canadian

Le Bény-Bocage · XXX · XII · XXX

Morteaux-Couliboeuf · XXXX

Etouvy · XXX · XXX · Damblainville · XXX · 5

Chenedolle · Falaise · I SS

Vire · Vassy · Condé-sur-Noireau · XXXX · 7 · XXXXX · Trun

Gathemo · XXX · VIII · Athis · XXX · LXXIV · XXX · Dives

Tinchebray · XXX · II · XXX · II SS · Putanges · B · Eberbach · Argentan

Flers · XXX · LXXXIV · XXX · XLVII · XXX · V · Ecouché

XXXX · 1 · XXX · XIX · Briouze · XXXX · 3

■ *Above:* All the German units trapped inside the Falaise Pocket were understrength, and short of fuel and ammunition.

During the early hours of 20 August, *Das Reich* scraped together its last 20 tanks to launch a final attack to keep the escape route open. All day the Waffen-SS men battled to keep the Polish 1st Armoured Division at bay, thereby allowing the trapped *Hitlerjugend* and *Leibstandarte* Kampfgruppen to reach safety. Inside one of their armoured halftracks was the badly wounded Hausser, who had lost an eye during an artillery strike. It took the Allies two days to clean up the remnants of resistance inside the Kessel, taking 50,000 prisoners and finding 10,000 dead Germans in the carnage. More than 3000 vehicles had been left behind, including 187 tanks, 252 artillery pieces, 157 light armoured vehicles, 1778 trucks and 669 staff cars.

### Waffen-SS casualties controversy

Controversy surrounds the casualties inflicted on the Waffen-SS divisions during this terrible ordeal, with some sources trying to claim they were reduced to little more than a few thousand men each. The *Hitlerjugend* reported its strength on 22 August as 12,500 men; *Leibstandarte* got away with 17,000 men; and *Das Reich* also reported being only

7000 men short, giving it a strength of 14–15,000 men. The two divisions of II SS Panzer Corps suffered a similar level of losses, around 5000 men each, for the whole Normandy campaign. By far the heaviest losses in the Normandy campaign were suffered by the 17th SS Division, which lost nearly 8000 men. The misreporting of the losses is due to two factors. Firstly, lightly wounded casualties were kept with divisions and returned to duty as soon as possible. Secondly, divisional commanders often only reported their "frontline" strength, rather than total manpower strength, as a means to pressure higher commanders to give them reinforcements. It is clear that the vast majority of the corps-level and divisional Waffen-SS administrative, supply and maintenance units escaped from the Falaise Kessel long before the Allied pincers snapped shut.

## Decimated panzer regiments

All the Waffen-SS panzer regiments were crippled during the Falaise battles. Few got away with more than 20 tanks, and Bittrich's corps reported on 21 August it had no operational tanks at all. More importantly, many vehicles under repair had to be abandoned in the pocket, meaning no replacement tanks could be returned to action. They would have to wait until they reached Germany to receive new vehicles.

Far more damage was done during the retreat across France to the German border in the last week of August and first two weeks of September. Allied air attacks and

■ *Above:* German supplies abandoned in Normandy, as Hitler's army begins its retreat through France.

■ *Below:* Inside the pocket the Americans found death and destruction.

ambushes by French and Belgian resistance fighters inflicted a steady stream of losses on the German convoys.

Hitler's idea of forming a new line on the Seine was a non-starter. Paris fell on 25 August following an uprising by the French resistance. Dietrich tried to form another line on the Somme with the *Leibstandarte, Das Reich* and *Hitlerjugend* Divisions a couple of days later, but it was soon outflanked and the divisions retreated back to Germany through the Ardennes region of Belgium.

Resistance fighters ambushed a number of their convoys, including one carrying Kurt Meyer on 6 September. The *Hitlerjugend*'s famous commander was captured and, realizing the value of their prize, the Belgians kept him alive and handed him over to the Allies.

II SS Panzer Corps fought a stiff rearguard action against the Americans near Cambrai on 2 September. The *Hohenstaufen*'s remaining 88mm guns were deployed to blunt a tank attack and allow the

> *Realizing the value of their prize, the Belgians kept Meyer alive and handed him over to the Allies*

rest of the corps to break free. The division's 32-year-old commander, SS-Obersturmbannführer Walther Harzer, remained behind to control the battle from his command halftrack. Harzer had taken over from the wounded Sylvester Stadler a few days earlier, and he was determined to make the Americans pay a heavy price for getting past his small Kampfgruppe. More than 200 Shermans appeared later on in the morning. Harzer's gunners engaged them at their maximum range of 3000m (3280yd) in order to inflict the maximum delay on the American pursuit. It worked.

It took the US GIs all day to get past the Waffen-SS lines, and they lost 40 tanks in the process. His mission accomplished, Harzer ordered a withdrawal, but found his small command group was cut off. For three days it was behind Allied lines, dodging between British tank columns and stealing petrol and other supplies until it made contact with German troops who were retreating through Brussels.

■ *Right:* On 25 August 1944, Paris fell to French resistance fighters after the German garrison commander refused to obey Hitler's orders to destroy the city's historic buildings.

The battered and tired remnants of the Waffen-SS panzers divisions were not welcomed back to Germany as heroes and given a well-earned rest. They were immediately told to get their units ready for action. Hitler was determined to continue fighting. *Ad hoc* Kampfgruppen were formed and sent to bolster the defences along the Third Reich's western frontier. The front was barely held together at all by the 24 infantry and 11 panzer "divisions" that Model had under his command on 29 August.

The Wehrmacht which was stationed in the West was now a shadow of the force Rommel had used in his attempt to beat back the Allied invasion in June. During the 10 weeks of fighting since the Allies had landed in Normandy, the German forces had lost 23,109 dead, 67,240 wounded and 198,616 missing or taken prisoner. Almost 1500 of the 2248 tanks sent to Normandy had been destroyed, decimated or captured by the Allies.

## Materiel superiority

Allied losses during this period had been as grim as those incurred by the Germans. They numbered 36,976 dead out of a total of 209,672 casualties. The Germans forces, in particular the Waffen-SS, had made the Allies pay dearly for their victory.

Nevertheless, ultimately the tactical skill and fighting spirit of men like Meyer and Wittmann had not been able to compensate for the overwhelming materiel superiority of the Allies.

■ *Above:* By the end of August, almost 200,000 Germans were in Allied prisoner-of-war cages in France. German defeat appeared total.

# CHAPTER 12

# FLESH AGAINST STEEL

## II SS Panzer Corps defeats Operation Market Garden.

I n the first week of September 1944, Willi Bittrich's II SS Panzer Corps was ordered to move to a reorganizing and refitting area north of the Dutch town of Arnhem. The unit had been in action continuously for just over two months, and was now desperately in need of a quiet period to get itself ready for battle again.

Plans were already in train to bring Bittrich's two divisions, the *Hohenstaufen* and *Frundsberg*, back up to strength, and Arnhem seemed like a good place to begin this time-consuming task. There they would be safe from Allied attack. Lightly wounded personnel were sent to hospitals in Germany in order to recover, and those in need of training were sent on courses in specialist depots.

Remaining in the Dutch barracks which had been taken over by the Waffen-SS corps were probably no more than 6000 men, who were equipped with whatever tanks, artillery and vehicles they had managed to bring with them out of France. No longer worthy of the title "division", the *Hohenstaufen* and *Frundsberg* were dubbed divisional Kampfgruppen. It was doubtful if the whole of the corps would be able to put more than 30 tanks or assault guns into the field.

Walther Harzer's *Hohenstaufen* was then ordered to move to Germany to be rebuilt there. Before it left, it was to hand over its

■ *Left:* British paratroopers captured by the *Hohenstaufen* Panzer Division during the bitter battle for Arnhem.

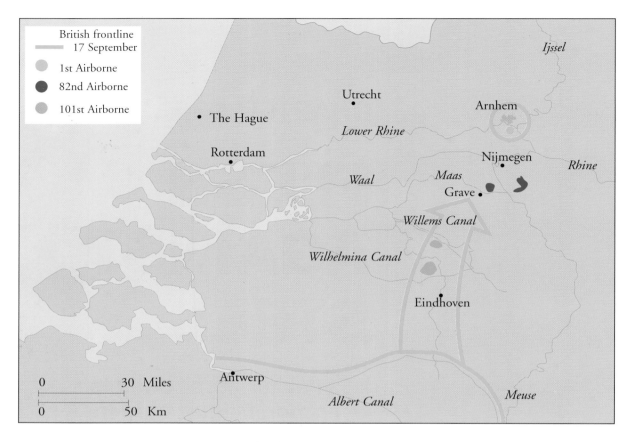

**Above:**
Montgomery's
Operation Market
Garden, which
aimed to finish the
war by the end of
1944. The coloured
shaded areas
represent the drop
zones for the three
airborne divisions
that took part.
The pink circle
represents
Montgomery's
main objective.

remaining operational vehicles and heavy weapons to Heinz Harmel's *Frundsberg*, which was to remain in Holland. At the same time as this reorganization process was under way, contingency orders were issued stating that the two units were to be prepared to dispatch "alarm" Kampfgruppen to crisis zones. Not believing intelligence reports that the Allied advance had run out of steam, Harzer decided to keep hold of many of his precious remaining tanks and heavy weapons until the very last minute, in case he had to send his men into battle. He simply ordered their tracks to be removed so they would be classed as non-operational and therefore exempt from the transfer instructions.

The conventional organization of both divisions had all but collapsed. Instead, the remaining troops were grouped into a number of *ad hoc* Kampfgruppen. Harmel gutted his panzergrenadier heavy weapons companies to form the division's only antitank gun company. Likewise, all the armoured half-tracks in the division were grouped in the

reconnaissance battalion to provide him with a powerful strike force. The artillery regiment's self-propelled gun drivers and crews were all transferred to the panzer regiment, and all the infantry were combined into three weak panzergrenadier battalions.

## Building the front at Eindhoven

What new equipment had arrived – mainly 15 Panzerjäger IV self-propelled guns – had been dispatched to the Dutch-Belgian border, under the command of Kampfgruppe *Hienke*. This was formed around one of *Frundsberg's* panzergrenadier battalions, an engineer and reconnaissance company. *Hohenstaufen* was ordered to provide an additional panzergrenadier battalion for this force, which was helping to build up the front south of the Dutch city of Eindhoven. It was increasingly involved in a series of inconclusive engagements along the border, and was sent into action in a futile attack against the Neerpelt bridgehead on 15 September, in which three of the Panzerjäger IVs were knocked out.

Harzer, although preoccupied with preparing to move his division by train to Germany, ordered his troops to form 19 company sized quick-reaction infantry Kampfgruppen. Much of his divisional equipment was being loaded on trains when the first Allied airborne landings occurred. His division was the closest to Arnhem itself, with the *Frundsberg* Division garrisoned farther to the north and west near Apeldoorn.

*By September, the Allied armies in France and Belgium had largely outrun their supply lines*

Also in the Arnhem area were two other Waffen-SS units, which were not under II SS Panzer Corps command. Major Sepp Krafft commanded a Waffen-SS noncommissioned training depot to the west of Arnhem itself, and in the outskirts there was also a 600-strong battalion of Dutch Waffen-SS infantry.

Bittrich had his headquarters in a small village nearly 10km (6.2 miles) to the east of Arnhem where, in between planning the rebuilding of his corps, he would fume about how the Führer had lost the war. Once an ardent Nazi who had transferred to the Waffen-SS from the army, Bittrich was now thoroughly disillusioned with the war, and was particularly unhappy when several of his old army comrades were arrested and executed after the 20 July Bomb Plot. He, however, remained a very professional officer. His corps headquarters remained largely intact, and Bittrich had enough military pride left to ensure no one could accuse him of being unprofessional. If II SS Panzer Corps was called to fight, it would give a good account of itself.

In Arnhem's Tafelberg Hotel, Field Marshal Walther Model was trying to patch together his hopelessly undermanned and under-equipped army group to defend the northwest border of Germany. He had a reputation of being a great improviser and, after his successes on the Eastern Front, was nicknamed the "Führer's Fireman". Even at this point of the war, he was still ultra-loyal to Hitler and could still be counted on to follow the Führer's orders to the letter. He was sitting down to lunch on 17 September with his staff when hundreds of aircraft were heard flying overhead. Operation Market Garden had begun.

By the beginning of September, the Allied armies in France and Belgium had largely outrun their supply lines, which stretched all the way back to the Normandy beaches. The Germans had destroyed or still held every port on the French Atlantic coast, and the approaches to the huge Belgian port of Antwerp were still covered by German guns. With only a fraction of the needed supplies coming ashore, the Allied armies could no longer advance into Germany on a wide front. The recently promoted Field Marshal Montgomery successfully lobbied the Allied supreme commander, Eisenhower, to allow him to drive into Holland to seize bridges over the Rhine, and then turn right to advance into Germany's industrial heartland of the Ruhr.

## Multiple airdrop

The normally cautious Montgomery now came up with a very ambitious and daring plan to capture the strategic bridge across the Rhine at Arnhem with a parachute drop by the British 1st Airborne Division. The US 82nd and 101st Airborne Divisions would also be dropped to seize the bridges across the Waal and Maas rivers, as well as the Willems and Wilhelmina canals, to allow the tanks of the British XXX Corps to motor 103km (64 miles) up from Belgium to relieve the troops on Arnhem bridge. In total some 35,000 Allied paratroopers and glider-borne troops would be dropped in the largest airborne operation in military history. Lieutenant-General Brian Horrocks would predict that his XXX Corps would be in Arnhem in 60 hours.

The official history of General Eisenhower's headquarters wrote of Operation Market Garden:

"It seemed to fit the pattern of current Allied strategy. It conformed to General Arnold's recommendation for an operation some distance east of the enemy's forward positions and beyond the area where enemy

■ **Above:**
**Lieutenant-General Brian Horrocks (centre) was put in charge of punching through to relieve the Allied airborne divisions holding key bridges in Holland.**

more easterly approaches, and would carry us to an area relatively remote from the Ruhr.' He considered that these were overridden by certain major advantages: (1) the operation would outflank the Siegfried Line defences; (2) it would be on the line which the enemy would consider the least likely for the Allies to use; and (3) the area was the one with the easiest range for the Allied airborne forces."

When RAF reconnaissance Spitfires photographed German tanks near Arnhem, the deputy commander of the First Airborne Army, Lieutenant-General Frederick "Boy" Browning, ignored the intelligence. Other Allied intelligence officers discounted the idea that the remnants of II SS Panzer Corps could put up serious resistance. The party was on, and nothing was going to spoil the show – except Bittrich's panzer troops.

Allied bombers and fighter-bombers hit targets all over southern Holland during the morning of 17 September, but the veteran Waffen-SS men took little notice. They had been bombed and strafed on a daily basis for the past two months, so it had lost its novelty. Harzer even went ahead with a ceremony to present the Knight's Cross to the commander of his reconnaissance battalion, SS-Hauptsturmführer Viktor Graebner. After 13:00 hours, when the first British paratroopers started to land to the west of Arnhem, Bittrich swung into action, alerting his troops with a warning order that was issued at 13:40 hours. With these brief orders he set in train the German counteroffensive

reserves were normally located; it afforded an opportunity for using the long-idle airborne resources; it was in accord with Field Marshal Montgomery's desire for a thrust north of the Rhine while the enemy was disorganized; it would help reorient the Allied drive in the direction 21st Army Group thought it should go; and it appeared to General Eisenhower to be the boldest and best move the Allies could make at the moment. The Supreme Commander realized that the momentum of the drive into Germany was being lost and thought that by this action it might be possible to get a bridgehead across the Rhine before the Allies were stopped. The airborne divisions, he knew, were in good condition and could be supported without throwing a crushing burden on the already overstrained supply lines. At worst, General Eisenhower thought the operation would strengthen the 21st Army Group in its later fight to clear the Schelde estuary. Field Marshal Montgomery examined the objections that the proposed route of advance 'involved the additional obstacle of the Lower Rhine ... as compared with

> *The Supreme Commander realized the momentum of the drive into Germany was being lost*

that was to defeat Operation Market Garden. Harzer was ordered to assemble his Kampfgruppen and move with "absolute speed" to contain and defeat the British airborne Oosterbeek landing. Meanwhile, the *Frundsberg* Division was to race south and hold the Nijmegen bridges across the Waal to stop reinforcements reaching Arnhem.

Within minutes of receiving their orders, Waffen-SS units sprang into action. Harzer's men began moving into the town by whatever means they found: trucks, tanks, halftracks, cars, trams, even bicycles. SS-Obersturm-bannführer Ludwig Spindler, commander of the division's artillery regiment, was given command of the Kampfgruppe that would hold the western edge of Arnhem. At the same time its tank, artillery and reconnaissance units began getting the vehicles that had been deliberately put out of action to stop them being transferred to the *Frundsberg* Division into some semblance of

working order. In two hours, his 400 men and 40 vehicles were rolling out of their camp towards Arnhem town centre. They had orders to move ahead of the *Frundsberg* and secure Nijmegen bridge.

On the drop zones west of Arnhem, 8000 British troops were forming up and preparing to move off to their objectives. Within minutes, Krafft's trainee NCOs were in action, fighting in the forests around the

■ *Below:* German prisoners captured by American paratroopers during their assault on Nijmegen.

■ *Above:*
**Determined and quick thinking by the men of II SS Panzer Corps thwarted Operation Market Garden, resulting in heavy Allied losses.**

eral blocks of buildings nearby. Harmel was away in Berlin arranging for new equipment for his division, so his chief of staff, SS-Sturmbannführer Paetsch, issued orders for the units heading to Nijmegen to be diverted to an improvised ferry across the Rhine that had been established upstream from Arnhem at Pannerden. Brinkmann was told to do what he could to contain the British on the north bank of Rhine and prevent further reinforcements from reaching the bridge. He set about his task with relish.

Far to the south, Kampfgruppe *Heinke* was soon in action against XXX Corps' Guards Armoured Division as it pushed up the main road towards Eindhoven. Artillery barrages and air strikes smashed the German paratroopers defending the road, and when the Waffen-SS Panzerjäger IVs tried to help, several were knocked out. British Shermans were soon streaming northwards.

Heavy fighting now raged all around Arnhem as Harzer threw more and more troops into action to stop the British establishing a firm base. Speed of response was more important than strength or coordination. It was imperative that the British be denied the chance to establish themselves in firm positions. Spindler first threw two companies of artillerymen, fighting as infantrymen, into action during the evening of 17 September. Two bigger infantry Kampfgruppen then joined the battle. The following day, two more Kampfgruppen arrived, along with the first tanks and assault guns from the *Hohenstaufen*, as well as army units. The battle for Arnhem bridge burst into life on the morning of the 18th, when

British drop zones, delaying their advance for vital hours. One British airborne unit, the 2nd Battalion, the Parachute Regiment (2 PARA), slipped past Krafft's men and was soon marching into the town centre. Minutes before 2 PARA reached Arnhem bridge, Graebner's column raced across the huge structure and within an hour the men were in Nijmegen. An improvised Luftwaffe and police Kampfgruppe had already secured the strategic bridge and Graebner had little to do. The *Frundsberg* Division was equally quick off the mark, and its reconnaissance battalion, under SS-Sturmbannführer Brinkmann, was on its way to Nijmegen. As the column of armoured halftracks approached Arnhem bridge, it came under fire from British paratroopers. 2 PARA now held the northern edge of the bridge and sev-

the British paratroopers heard a column of tracked armoured vehicles approaching. Graebner, being an aggressive and self-confident officer, had heard that British troops had cut him off in Nijmegen and, on his own initiative, had returned to clear the bridge for reinforcements. This was to be a *coup de main* raid to take the British by surprise and scatter them by shock action. Waffen-SS armoured halftracks, Puma armoured cars, Volkswagen jeeps and

> *Graebner's column raced across Arnhem bridge and within an hour the men were in Nijmegen*

Graebner's captured British Humber scout car raced over Arnhem bridge at 48km/h (30mph), with Waffen-SS troopers training their machine guns and rifles on the high buildings overlooking the elevated highway. Two vehicles got across the bridge unscathed and then the British Paras opened fire. Machine guns, mortars, PIAT bazookas, Sten guns and rifles raked the column. One halftrack took a direct hit and veered out of control before turning over. Other vehicles went out of control, crashing into each other and effectively blocking the road. Two vehi-

cles crashed over the side of the elevated road. A handful of Waffen-SS men in the tangled wreckage tried to return fire. For almost two hours the carnage continued, until at last the remnants of Graebner's force pulled back to safety at the southern edge of the bridge, leaving 12 wrecked vehicles behind. Scores of the reconnaissance men were dead, including their commander.

### Prising out the Paras

The British Paras were not going to be removed easily. Army panzers were brought

■ *Below:* Captured Waffen-SS men are put to work by their British captors during the early phase of Market Garden.

up to reinforce Brinkmann's Kampfgruppe, and a determined effort was launched to blast out the British. As the battle was raging at Arnhem bridge, Spindler was continuing his effort to hold the 1st Airborne Division, which was pushing eastwards to help their comrades in the centre of the town. Spindler's force had grown to 1000 men in several independent Kampfgruppen, backed by 30 tanks. An *ad hoc* division of army and Waffen-SS units was also trying to build a front to block the British move westwards and to seal them in a Kessel. The Germans were closing in.

During the morning of 18 September, Harmel returned to Arnhem and quickly received his orders from Bittrich, who declared: "Schwerpunkt (main effort) is south." No effort was to be spared to hold Nijmegen bridge and prevent a link-up between the British tanks and their airborne troops. All night his troops had been labouring to get the Pannerden ferry working and, by late morning, Waffen-SS engineers on trucks and riding bicycles at last reached Nijmegen. They immediately began preparing it for demolition. At midday, SS-Hauptsturmführer Karl Heinz Euling arrived to assume command of the bridge defence Kampfgruppe. Soon, armoured half-tracks, mortars and four Panzerjäger IVs were rumbling over Nijmegen bridge. Artillery batteries were established on the north bank of the Waal to provide support.

## Army and Waffen-SS units were trying to build a front to block the British move westwards

### Laying the trap

When American paratroopers edged into Nijmegen they were met with a heavy barrage of German artillery and mortar fire, sending them scurrying back to seek cover. More *Frundsberg* reinforcements arrived during the day, and Euling's men began laying minefields and barbed wire, as well as building field fortifications. Harmel set up his command post on the north bank of the Waal, from where he could observe the key bridge. Model relayed to him the Führer's orders that the bridges were not be blown, but held to allow a German counterattack to restore the front along the Dutch–Belgian border. Harmel was having none of this nonsense, though, and was determined to order the bridge to be blown if British tanks attempted to cross. Late in the afternoon, German observation posts south of Nijmegen reported British tanks operating with the American paratroopers.

Throughout the afternoon and into the night of 18/19 September, fighting raged in Arnhem. Tiger tanks were brought up to blast the paratroopers on Arnhem bridge and the army's 280th Assault Gun Brigade arrived to support Spindler's drive against the main British force. Slowly, the Germans were becoming more organized and effective. A

■ *Below:* The British Guards Armoured Division spearheaded the drive to relieve the airborne troops trapped north of the Rhine at Arnhem. These men are members of the Irish Guards.

concerted defence line was established and the first counterattacks were launched. Losses were heavy on both sides, with most German Kampfgruppen losing 50 percent casualties. The German armour was decisive, allowing the outnumbered Waffen-SS Kampfgruppen to stand off and blast the British out of their positions.

The date 20 September signified the decisive phase in the battle. The Guards Armoured Division had linked up with the 82nd Airborne Division and planned to seize the Nijmegen bridge during the day. Harmel

had some 500 Waffen-SS troopers in the town fighting alongside a similar number of Luftwaffe, army and police troops. 88mm and 37mm Flak guns were emplaced in order to protect the large road ramps leading up to the bridge, and the Panzerjäger IVs were also in the town.

### All-day bombardment

British guns bombarded the German positions throughout the day, and American paratroopers and British Grenadier Guards edged into the suburbs of Nijmegen. The

■ *Above:* **Waffen-SS troops quickly built a firm defence line, trapping the British 1st Airborne Division in a small pocket at Oosterbeek, west of Arnhem town centre.**

■ *Above:* A patrol from the *Hohenstaufen* Division hunts down an isolated group of British paratroopers in the suburbs of Arnhem.

bombardment knocked out the key 88mm Flak guns that provided the main defence of the bridge approach routes. In the afternoon 40 British tanks moved up to the riverbank and started to fire smoke shells onto the far bank to the west of the bridge. A battalion of US paratroopers then raced forward with canvas assault boats and set course for the northern bank of the Waal. German mortars and 20mm Flak guns raked the boats, killing or wounding half the Americans, but they kept going through the maelstrom. Once

ashore, they scattered the few old men and boy soldiers holding the rear end of the bridge. As the river assault was under way, a squadron of British tanks rushed the southern edge of the bridge. Several tanks fell to Panzerfaust fire from the Waffen-SS men. The tanks just kept moving and, within minutes, were up on the bridge, machine-gunning the *Frundsberg* engineers who were still placing demolition charges. American paratroopers followed close behind. Watching horrified from his command post,

Harmel immediately ordered the bridge to be blown. The engineer officer kept pressing the detonation switch. Nothing happened. Artillery fire had damaged the initiation cable; Nijmegen bridge was in British hands. Harmel was dismayed; the road to Arnhem seemed open, yet the Shermans just stopped. They had run out of fuel and ammunition and needed replenishment. Also, more infantry were needed to clear the villages along the single road north to Arnhem, otherwise German guns would be able to pick off the British tanks with ease.

### Dash for freedom

The vital British infantry were still stuck in Nijmegen, fighting Euling's men. During the night the Waffen-SS officer gathered 100 or so of his remaining men together and made an escape bid. As they listened to more

British tanks rolling over the Nijmegen bridge, Euling led his men on the walkway underneath it to the north bank and safety. They had put up determined resistance and delayed the British at a decisive moment in the battle. The price for this success was high. More than 260 German bodies were found in the ruins of Nijmegen.

On Arnhem bridge itself, meanwhile, 2 PARA was on its last legs. Out of ammunition and with almost every soldier dead or wounded, including its commanding officer, Lieutenant-Colonel Johnny Frost, the battalion surrendered during the morning of 21 September. They had no idea XXX Corps tanks were only 17km (10.5 miles) away. Thus ended an epic battle.

Even before the remains of Graebner's vehicles had been removed from Arnhem bridge, reinforcements were on their way to

■ *Right:* German armour was brought up finally to "liquidate" the trapped British paratroopers holding Arnhem bridge.

■ *Below:* As Polish paratroopers landed on their drop zone south of Arnhem, Waffen-SS troops were waiting and inflicted heavy losses.

help Harmel block any further move north by the British armour. Four StuG IIIs and 16 Panzer IVs of *Frundsberg*'s Panzer Regiment had been ferried across the Rhine on 20 September and, by the early hours of the following morning, had set up a "stop line" north of Nijmegen. The whole of the "island" between Arnhem and Nijmegen was low-lying marsh or prone to flooding. Any

kind of movement off roads was impossible for tanks or wheeled vehicles, and very difficult for infantrymen. Harmel skilfully placed his forces to dominate the road from Nijmegen to Arnhem. British fears about being picked off on the raised road by German antitank fire were found to be fully justified when the Guards Armoured began advancing at 11:00 hours. When the first

■ *Right:* The Waffen-SS successfully blocked the highway between Arnhem and Nijmegen, and thus doomed 2 PARA.

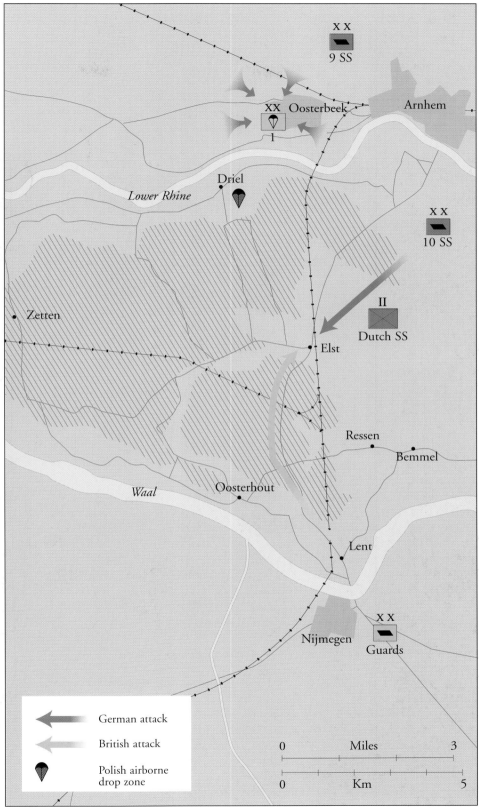

X X
9 SS

XX Oosterbeek                Arnhem
1

*Lower Rhine*          Driel

X X
10 SS

Zetten

II
Dutch SS

Elst

Ressen
Bemmel

*Waal*          Oosterhout

Lent

X X

Nijmegen          Guards

German attack

British attack

Polish airborne
drop zone

0          Miles          3

0          Km          5

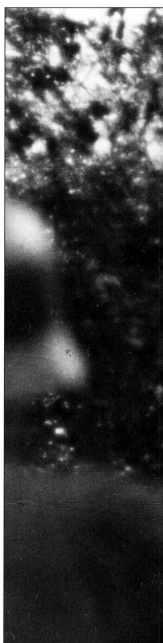

■ *Left:* StuG III assault guns provided close support to Waffen-SS assault troops during the final stages of the battle.

Irish Guards Sherman reached the outskirts of the village of Elst, a high-velocity 75mm round blew the tank's tracks off. More guns opened fire and four tanks were soon blazing on the road, which was now blocked. British infantry tried to attack across the open fields but were soon pinned down by Harmel's artillery. At midday on 21 September, eight Panther tanks led columns of *Frundsberg* panzergrenadiers across Arnhem bridge and moved to join Harmel's depleted Kampfgruppe north of Nijmegen bridge. With the arrival of these reinforcements, any chance the Allies had of reaching Arnhem was doomed.

## Out of Arnhem

Harzer's troops continued to press back the eastern flank of the British force east of Arnhem. He ordered his Kampfgruppe to form small penetration teams, each led by a couple of StuG IIIs, to push forward into the British lines. In addition, more guns were brought up to blast the British.

South of the Rhine, a brigade of Polish paratroopers was dropped just behind the *Frundsberg's* "stop line". With customary promptness, Harmel reorganized his small Kampfgruppen to contain the new landing. A battalion of sailors was thrown in to hold the Poles and 16 88mm Flak guns were positioned to cover the road from Nijmegen. Batteries of Nebelwerfers were brought up to stop the Poles massing for infantry attacks. Every attempt to break through his line was rebuffed with heavy losses.

The Germans were not content just to block the Allied advance south of Arnhem. XXX Corps relied on supplies coming up the single road from Belgium to ensure it could keep pushing north. Model was determined to cut this road, which was known as the "corridor". The Waffen-SS Kampfgruppe that had been brushed aside in the first XXX Corps attack south of Eindhoven had been re-equipped and reorganized by 22 September. Its Panzerjäger IVs led a major attack on the corridor at Veghel that briefly cut XXX Corps' lifeline. American paratroopers counterattacked, driving them off, but for several hours the corridor was closed. II SS Panzer Corps had more valuable time to beef up its "stop line" south of Arnhem.

## King Tigers for Bittrich

The 1st Airborne Division continued to hold out in the face of continuous German attacks. During the night of 23/24 September, 45 army King Tiger tanks arrived to help Bittrich. He sent 30 south to help Harmel stop the Guards Armoured Division, and the rest turned westwards towards the Oosterbeek Kessel. There they were used to blast British strongpoints with spectacular effect. Determined groups of paratroopers, however, managed to knock some out with

■ *Below:* Vicious street fighting raged as the British 1st Airborne Division tried to hold onto to its precarious bridgehead north of the Rhine.

their PIAT bazookas at almost point-blank range. By 25 September, some 110 German guns were ringing Oosterbeek, bombarding the British trenches. RAF transport planes that tried to drop supplies to the beleaguered garrison had to fly through a wall of heavy Flak fire. Many of the supplies that were dropped ended up in the hands of Bittrich's men because they had captured the British drop zones.

A "final attack" was ordered by Bittrich for 25 September. Four *Hohenstaufen* Kampfgruppen made good progress, thanks to heavy King Tiger support, and one unit broke through the now depleted defences and overran a British artillery battery. Realizing that his 1st Airborne Division was on its last legs, Montgomery authorized its withdrawal during the night. After swimming across the Rhine to a precarious bridgehead held by the Poles, by dawn just under 2500 men had escaped. Bittrich's men advanced cautiously through the ruins of the Oosterbeek Kessel. They rounded up some 6000 prisoners, the majority of whom were wounded, and buried more than 1000 dead

■ *Below:* A dead Waffen-SS pioneer during the operation to wire Nijmegen bridge for demolition. The *Frundsberg*'s battle to hold up the British armour here effectively sealed the fate of the paratroopers trapped in Arnhem.

British soldiers. The Americans lost another 3000 men and XXX Corps lost 1500 men, as well as 70 tanks. Bittrich's men were in awe of the fighting qualities of their British opponents, and the formalities of the Geneva Convention were generally observed during the battle. There were no accusations of the premeditated killing of prisoners that had sullied the reputation of Waffen-SS units in Normandy and later in the Ardennes,

The German losses were equally heavy. Some 8000 German casualties were recorded for all the units engaged during Market Garden, from Eindhoven to Arnhem. In the Arnhem area, more than 3000 casualties were inflicted on German units and 1725 of these were dead. The majority of these casualties were incurred by Bittrich's units.

Bittrich's men, however, had defeated Montgomery's daring bid to end the war by Christmas 1944. The prompt reaction of the Waffen-SS panzer corps had ensured the key bridge at Nijmegen was defended and then the road to Arnhem blocked. This was the vital ground of Market Garden. Bittrich had spotted this in his orders which were issued within minutes of the first Allied paratroops landing. For the next week, he ensured his Schwerpunkt remained firmly in German hands. No matter how bravely the British

paratroopers fought in Arnhem, they were doomed as soon as Harmel's Kampfgruppe took up defensive positions on Nijmegen bridge on 18 September.

Senior British intelligence officer Brian Urquhart had this to say of Arnhem: "My job as chief intelligence officer was to try to evaluate what the enemy reactions were going to be and how our troops ought to deal with them. The British airborne troops were going to be dropped at the far end of the operation at Arnhem – it was across the third bridge, so there were three bridges that had to be captured before you got to the British airborne troops. I became increasingly alarmed, first of all at the German preparations, because there were intelligence reports that there were two SS panzer divisions right next to where the British troops were to be dropped. These were the star troops of the German Army, the 10th and the 9th SS Panzer Divisions. They had been very badly mauled in Normandy and were refitting in this area. These were the best fighting troops in the German Army and they had heavy tanks. Airborne troops in those days had absolutely nothing.... They had limited supplies of ammunition, and they could not fight heavy armour because they didn't have the weapons to do it."

# CHAPTER 13

# SIXTH PANZER ARMY

## Building the army for Hitler's Ardennes Offensive.

**E**ver the optimist, Hitler was already thinking about how he could regain the initiative in the war even before the last remnants of his battered armies had retreated across the German and Dutch borders in September 1944. Hitler decided that his élite Waffen-SS panzer divisions would lead this new offensive. For reasons of secrecy, none of his top Wehrmacht commanders was let in on the secret. Each one was just told to get his troops ready for battle as soon as possible.

The 20 July Bomb Plot had destroyed for good Hitler's trust in the army's generals. He wanted his favourite Waffen-SS general, "Sepp" Dietrich, to command the most powerful armoured force Nazi Germany had ever put in the field. At an audience with the Führer in early September 1944, Dietrich was told that he was to command the newly formed Sixth Panzer Army. Although nominally an army formation – rebuilt from the remnants of XII Corps that had been badly mauled in Russia during the summer – almost all of Dietrich's key staff officers were old hands from either his *Leibstandarte* or I SS Panzer Corps days. Dietrich's right-hand man was SS-Brigadeführer Fritz Kraemer who, as chief of staff, was the powerhouse behind his commander's bluster. As an army commander,

■ *Left:* Monster Tiger II tanks were issued to the Waffen-SS for the first time during the build-up to the Battle of the Bulge.

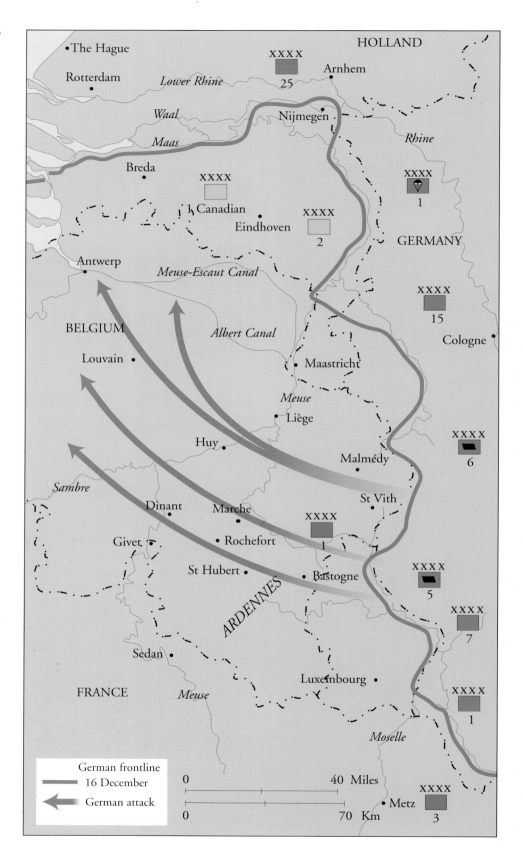

■ *Right:* On paper, the Ardennes attack seemed simple enough: a strike through the forests of the Ardennes to take Antwerp and split the Americans and the British.

The Hague
Rotterdam
HOLLAND
*Lower Rhine*
Arnhem
XXXX 25
*Waal*
*Maas*
Nijmegen
*Rhine*
GERMANY
Breda
XXXX
1
1 Canadian
XXXX
Eindhoven
XXXX 2
Antwerp
*Meuse-Escaut Canal*
BELGIUM
XXXX 15
Cologne
Louvain
*Albert Canal*
Maastricht
*Meuse*
Liège
XXXX 6
Huy
Malmédy
*Sambre*
St Vith
Dinant
Marche
XXXX 1
Givet
Rochefort
St Hubert
Bastogne
XXXX 5
ARDENNES
XXXX 7
Sedan
Luxembourg
FRANCE
*Meuse*
XXXX 1
*Moselle*

German frontline 16 December
German attack

0        40 Miles
0        70 Km

Metz
XXXX 3

Dietrich was perhaps over-promoted. He himself realized that he was no professional staff officer, and he relied on the likes of Kraemer to turn his ideas into concrete plans. Dietrich's true *forte* was man-management and motivation of the troops. His down-to-earth bonhomie was exactly what was needed to mould the thousands of new recruits who were now arriving to fill out the ranks of his divisions. Hitler liked him so much because Dietrich never had any ambition, beyond looking after his men. He never felt threatened by Dietrich and, because of their time together in 1920s Munich, the Führer would listen to his views on what was happening at the front.

To fill out his new army, Dietrich was given the two premier Waffen-SS corps headquarters, I SS and II SS Panzer Corps. I SS Panzer Corps boasted the *Leibstandarte* and *Hitlerjugend* Divisions, under the command of SS-Gruppenführer Hermann Priess, who had previously commanded the infamous Waffen-SS *Totenkopf* Panzer Division in Russia and was considered a sound tactician, if ruthless, even judging by Waffen-SS standards.

After his success commanding one of *Hitlerjugend*'s panzergrenadier regiments in Normandy, Wilhelm Mohnke, now an SS-Oberführer, was given the honour of commanding the *Leibstandarte*. Although

■ *Below:* US troops advanced into Germany during September 1944, capturing many of the old West Wall fortifications.

■ *Above:*
**Destruction of
communications
links hampered the
Allied build-up for
the invasion of
Germany during the
autumn of 1944,
giving Hitler his
chance to rebuild
his panzer reserves.**

Mohnke had fought well in Normandy, he was far from popular with his comrades. He lost a foot in the Yugoslav campaign, so missed fighting with Hausser's SS Panzer Corps in Russia, and he was still considered an "outsider" by many of the Waffen-SS officers who were now regimental and divisional commanders in Dietrich's army. Taking the place of Kurt Meyer, who had been captured in early September, was SS-Standartenführer Hugo Kraas, a highly decorated *Leibstandarte* Division veteran.

### Manpower changes

The victor of Arnhem, Willi Bittrich, remained in command of his beloved II SS Panzer Corps, and he had Walther Harzer at his side as chief of staff. He still had the *Hohenstaufen* Division, under the capable Sylvester Stadler, but the *Frundsberg* Division had been replaced by the *Das Reich* Division. Its commander, Heinz Lammerding, was a rabid Nazi who was considered one of the most stupid officers who ever reached high

command in the Waffen-SS. He relied on his chief of staff and regimental commanders to come up with battle plans and he was loathed for taking credit for their successes. Bittrich's corps, however, was now very strong and considered the most militarily professional in the Waffen-SS.

By the beginning of October, battered Waffen-SS units were garrisoned in old Wehrmacht barracks in northwest Germany, where they began to receive a steady stream of new recruits and new equipment. Thousands of conscripts, ex-Luftwaffe and navy men – as well as a few idealistic volunteers – had to be given the basics of military training and then moulded into effective fighting units. Under the direction of veteran officers, as well as noncommissioned officers, this process gathered pace during October and into November as more ambitious tank-gunnery training and field exercises were undertaken.

The presence of so many highly decorated combat veterans in the ranks of the

Waffen-SS panzer divisions was a major boost to morale. The newly arrived youngsters were treated to a series of medal parades, where Normandy veterans received decorations for their heroism only a few weeks before.

## Optimism against all odds

The steady arrival of new tanks, halftracks, artillery pieces, weapons and uniforms added to the spirit of optimism. If Germany, after five years of war, could still find the equipment to outfit completely four panzer divisions, then the Führer's promises of new wonder-weapons to turn the tide of war might well be true. By mid-November 1944,

morale among the divisions of Dietrich's new army was high and still rising.

Hitler ordered that Dietrich's army would have priority for new equipment coming from the Reich's remaining armament's factories. British and American bombing, along with the loss of factories in eastern Poland, meant this was almost the last efforts of armament minister Albert Speer's organization.

The reorganization and re-equipping of Dietrich's divisions was nearly complete by the end of November. While the frontline panzer divisions were at between 80 percent and 90 percent strength, there was a severe shortage of Waffen-SS corps-level artillery

■ *Below:* The new Jagdpanthers served in an army antitank battalion that was attached to the *Hitlerjugend* Division.

■ *Above:* The Tiger
II was a powerfully
armed tank but it
had limited mobility,
making it far from
ideal for use in the
mountainous terrain
of the Ardennes.

and heavy tank units. These had to be replaced by army units.

As befitted its status as one of the premier units of the Waffen-SS, the *Leibstandarte* boasted a formidable compliment of tanks and armoured vehicles. Its Panzer Regiment was again commanded by Jochen Peiper, who had now recovered from wounds received in Normandy, and fielded 38 Panthers and 34 Panzer IVs in a single battalion. To beef up its firepower, the 501st SS Heavy Panzer Battalion – formed from the old 101st SS Battalion – was attached with 30 of the monster 70-tonne (69-ton) King Tiger tanks. The division's antitank battalion boasted 21 Panzerjäger IVs. The division had the pick of Germany's manpower, and veteran officers considered it to be on a par with previous intakes.

### *Hitlerjugend*'s materiel

The *Hitlerjugend* Division was equally powerful, with 38 Panthers and 37 Panzer IVs in its Panzer Regiment, which were grouped in one battalion. It had a strong contingent of self-propelled antitank guns, including 22 Panzerjäger IVs, in its own antitank battalion. To add to its firepower, the army's 560th Antitank Battalion was attached to the Panzer Regiment, with 28 Panzerjäger IVs and 14 of the 88mm-armed Jagdpanthers. It continued to draw its recruits from the ranks of the Nazi Youth organization, which gave it its distinctive character.

I SS Panzer Corps had four army Nebelwerfer and two army artillery regiments attached for fire support.

Bittrich's II SS Panzer Corps was next in line to receive men and equipment, and was not as strong as its sister formation. He only had two army corps-level artillery regiments attached.

The *Das Reich* Division had 80 percent of its designated manpower strength and a strong compliment of armour. Its Panzer Regiment boasted two full battalions, with 58 Panthers, 28 Panzer IVs and 28 StuG IIIs. The division's antitank battalion had 20 Panzerjäger IVs.

The *Hohenstaufen* was the weakest Waffen-SS division, with only 75 percent of its allocated manpower under arms at the end of November 1944. Its Panzer Regiment had 35 Panthers and 28 StuG IIIs in one battalion and 39 Panzer IVs and 28 StuG IIIs in a second battalion. Antitank firepower was provided by 21 Panzerjäger IVs.

Dietrich had an assortment of army artillery, assault gun, antitank gun and heavy tank battalions attached to his army, which, when added to the divisional equipment totals, gave him just under 400 Panzer IV, King Tiger and Panther tanks, 685 guns, 340 rocket launchers, 112 assault guns and 215 Jagdpanzers.

One of the most unusual units attached to Dietrich's army was the 150th Panzer Brigade under the command of the flamboyant SS-Sturmbannführer Otto Skorzeny. It was intended to infiltrate behind Allied lines, dressed in US Army uniforms and driving American vehicles, in order to spread chaos and confusion. Some 500 Waffen-SS men were attached to this 2800-strong unit.

## The threat to the Reich

Building Dietrich's army was the number one priority for the Waffen-SS in the autumn of 1944, attracting the bulk of its resources and manpower. The Allied threat to the borders of the Reich was real, and a number of Waffen-SS panzer units, however, found themselves dragged into a series of small-scale engagements. The *Leibstandarte* Division dispatched two battalion-sized Kampfgruppen to help defend the city of

Aachen in early October when it was threatened by American troops. One of the Kampfgruppe was trapped inside the city when it was encircled. Rather than surrender with the rest of the army garrison, the Waffen-SS men broke out. Only eight soldiers made it back to German lines, though.

During October and November, the fight for Aachen became a bloody battle of attrition as the US Army tried to advance into the Hurtgen Forest and seize the Roer dams that provided power and water for the Ruhr industrial region. Stung that a German city had fallen into American hands, Hitler ordered defences to be strengthened. The *Frundsberg* Division was diverted from the effort to build up Dietrich's army to fight in the Aachen region.

■ *Left:* Dreadful winter weather proved Hitler's best ally, hiding the preparations for Operation Watch on the Rhine from Allied air reconnaissance.

The Alsace city of Metz on the French–German border was the scene of a similar bloody campaign during November 1944, as the famous General Patton tried to batter his way onto German territory. The 17th SS Panzergrenadier Division was sent to hold a stretch of the front south of Metz, and it gave Patton's 5th Infantry Division a stiff fight before being forced back to the West Wall at the end of November.

The determined resistance of the *Frundsberg* and 17th SS Divisions, along with scores of Wehrmacht divisions, was all part of Hitler's deception plan to cover his build-up for what was then known as Operation Watch on the Rhine. The strong defence of Metz and Aachen drew in Allied reserves and diverted their commanders' attention away from the Ardennes region in southeast Belgium.

**■ *Below:* Nearly four years of bombing meant German industry was reaching the limit of its endurance. The Ardennes attack would use up Germany's last reserves.**

> *The terrain was unsuitable for tanks, the roads were too narrow, their troops were not fully trained*

In September, even before Bittrich's II SS Panzer Corps had defeated Operation Market Garden, Hitler was thinking of launching a counteroffensive in the West. By early October, the Ardennes had been identified as the vulnerable point in the Allied line, with the port of Antwerp as the offensive's objective. The aim was to split the British forces in Holland from the American armies in France.

At the end of the month, Dietrich and the other army commanders who were to lead the offensive were briefed on the details of the plan. Even the normally loyal Dietrich was incredulous at what was being proposed. The terrain was unsuitable for tanks, the roads were too narrow, their troops were not yet fully trained and there was not enough fuel. They suggested a more modest offensive aimed at cutting off the American units in

Aachen, but the Führer was adamant. He wanted his dramatic and decisive attack, that would in one stroke change the course of the war. No argument was allowed.

A major deception programme was instituted to ensure that the Allies had no idea where the German offensive would fall. All orders were issued by hand at meetings, or by despatch rider, so Allied radio interception units would not be able to track the movement of headquarters concentrating for the coming offensive.

Apart from a few senior commanders, no one was briefed on the full scope of the operation in order to reduce the chance of it being compromised. Halfway through the planning of the attack, its codename was changed to Autumn Mist to further conceal its purpose. Even the Waffen-SS corps and division commanders were not briefed until 10 days before the offensive was due to start, and the troops themselves had no idea of the full size and scope of the operation until 24 hours before they were due to go into action. The German deception was totally successful, and the Allies were unaware about what was going to happen until the first panzers advanced into the Ardennes region. Surprise was total.

Hitler's greatest gamble finally got under way at 05:30 hours on 16 December 1944. He was relying on his Waffen-SS panzer élite to come forward and save his Thousand Year Reich, or die in the process.

■ *Above:* US Army Air Force B-17s pounded German factories by day, while the British RAF raided the Reich's cities by night.

# CHAPTER 14

# INTO THE ARDENNES

## Hitler's last great offensive in the West in December 1944.

Field Marshal Gerd von Rundstedt announced the following to his men in the West on the evening of 15 December 1944: "Soldiers of the West Front! Your great hour has arrived. Large attacking armies have started against the Anglo-Americans. I do not have to tell you anything more than that. You feel it yourself. WE GAMBLE EVERYTHING. You carry with you the holy obligation to give everything to achieve things beyond human possibilities for our Fatherland and our Führer!"

This stirring message was read to his attack troops as they moved up to their start-lines in the heavily wooded Eifel region of Germany. At 05:30 hours the following day, 1600 German guns and rocket launchers drenched the American frontline in deadly shrapnel. Then the first attack waves of infantry moved forward to clear a route for the panzer columns, who were to be unleashed to capture their first objective – the bridges across the Meuse – within 48 hours. The panzers would push on to Antwerp and victory.

"Sepp" Dietrich's Sixth Panzer Army was placed on the right flank of the assault and it would be the Schwerpunkt, or main effort, for the attack. I SS Panzer Corps would lead the advance to the Meuse, with II SS Panzer Corps following close behind. Once the vital river crossings were secure, Bittrich's divisions would spearhead the advance on Antwerp. To help Dietrich reach the bridges before the Americans had time to destroy them, Otto Skorzeny's special forces brigade – with small teams wearing US uniforms taking the

■ *Left:* *Leibstandarte* panzergrenadiers sweep through abandoned US Army vehicles in the opening of Operation Autumn Mist.

lead – was to race ahead of the Waffen-SS panzers and capture them in a *coup de main* operation. A regiment of Luftwaffe paratroopers was also to be dropped ahead of Dietrich's corps to capture a key road junction.

The sister *Leibstandarte* and *Hitlerjugend* Divisions would advance side-by-side towards the Meuse, after army Volksgrenadier divisions had cleared a way through the string of weak American units holding the front along the Belgian–German border. Once unleashed, the two divisions would race through the narrow forested valleys of the Ardennes until they reached the open countryside in the Meuse valley. The region's roads were winding and poorly maintained and, in most places, could barely take single-file traffic. The constricted road network in the Ardennes meant Dietrich's divisions had to be split up into self-contained columns, each of which was assigned its own specific route, or Rollbahn. All told, more than 6000 Waffen-SS vehicles had to be squeezed through the Ardennes road system. The speed of the Waffen-SS advance was determined as much by the commanders' traffic-control abilities as their tactical skills.

■ *Below:* The US Army's 14th Cavalry Group provided easy pickings for the *Leibstandarte*, which had smashed into the northern flank of the American defences.

The *Leibstandarte* Division was divided into three large Kampfgruppen, centred on the panzer regiment and its two panzer-grenadier regiments, and a "fast group" based on the division's reconnaissance battalion. *Hitlerjugend* was organized in the same way. The most powerful Kampfgruppe was Jochen Peiper's, which had all the *Leib-standarte*'s tanks, its King Tigers, a panzer-grenadier battalion carried in armoured half-tracks, and a battalion of army howitzers. All told, he had more than 5000 men, 117 tanks, 149 halftracks, 24 artillery pieces, 40 antiaircraft guns, and more than 500 other vehicles. It was the *Leibstandarte*'s lead unit and the success of the offensive would depend on its progress.

The atrocious road network meant that each division was allocated no more than two Rollbahns each, so their Kampfgruppen were lined up behind one another waiting for the lead troops to blast open a way forward. With little room for manoeuvre off-road, the lead Kampfgruppe was effectively reduced to relying on the handful of tanks it could place at its head to win through. Behind Peiper's Kampfgruppe were nose-to-tail columns of tanks and trucks.

### Traffic jams

Although the Germans had amassed more than 17 million litres (3.73 million UK gallons) of fuel to support the offensive, the jammed road network meant the troops at

■ *Above* Jochen Peiper's Kampfgruppe was boosted by the Tiger II tanks of the army's 501st Heavy Panzer Battalion for its drive westwards. Here, one of its tanks passes a column of captured GIs from the 99th Infantry Division.

the front of the convoys could not rely on refuelling tankers getting through to them. So Peiper and his colleagues in the lead Kampfgruppe were ordered to seize US petrol dumps to maintain the pace of their advance.

Hitler had wanted to launch the offensive in early November, but delays in massing the necessary troops and supplies had put it back until December. This brought with it one advantage: the fog, rain and low cloud that shrouded the Ardennes provided cover from the Allied fighter-bombers that had paralyzed German panzer columns in Normandy in the summer.

On the freezing night of 15 December, the *Leibstandarte* moved into its forward

assembly areas behind the sector of front held by the 12th Volksgrenadier and 3rd Parachute Divisions. These were units that had been decimated in Russia and Normandy, and then rapidly rebuilt with personnel from rear-echelon units. They lacked heavy equipment and trained infantry commanders. The *Hitlerjugend* was waiting a few kilometres to the north, behind the 277th Volksgrenadier Division.

## American resistance

The 12th and 3rd Divisions' attacks quickly stalled in the face of very determined, but poorly coordinated, American resistance. They were supposed to have captured the town of Losheim and its key road junction in a couple of hours, to allow Peiper's tanks to roar into action as dawn broke. Minefields held up the attack, and the two divisions were still fighting their way through American positions in the early afternoon. When a breach was opened, it was found a key bridge was blocked and a temporary one had to be built by army engineers. Furious at the delay, Peiper ordered his own Waffen-SS engineers to begin building their own. It was not until well after dark that his column got into Losheim, where Peiper was dismayed to find the commander of the lead parachute regiment had allowed his men to go to sleep, rather than press on with the advance. The determined Waffen-SS officer "took" the paratroopers under his command and they were soon loaded onto the back of his King

Tigers which pressed on into the night. Several tanks and vehicles were lost when the column ran into a minefield, but Peiper ordered the advance to continue regardless.

## Peiper's column presses on

All night Peiper's men forged on, with two Panthers leading the way until they surprised an American scout company parked up in a village just before dawn. Most of the GIs were captured and subsequently filmed by Nazi propaganda teams accompanying Peiper's column. The weather briefly cleared to allow some American fighters to attack, but they were unable to inflict much damage or delay the column. Running short of fuel, Peiper now made a diversion to raid a large US fuel dump. His tanks were soon being refuelled

■ *Below:* Battle-hardened Waffen-SS troopers cautiously move past vehicles abandoned by the poorly motivated GIs holding the line in the Ardennes.

**■ Right:** The Germans achieved total surprise, but the going was painfully slow, and soon the lead elements were behind schedule.

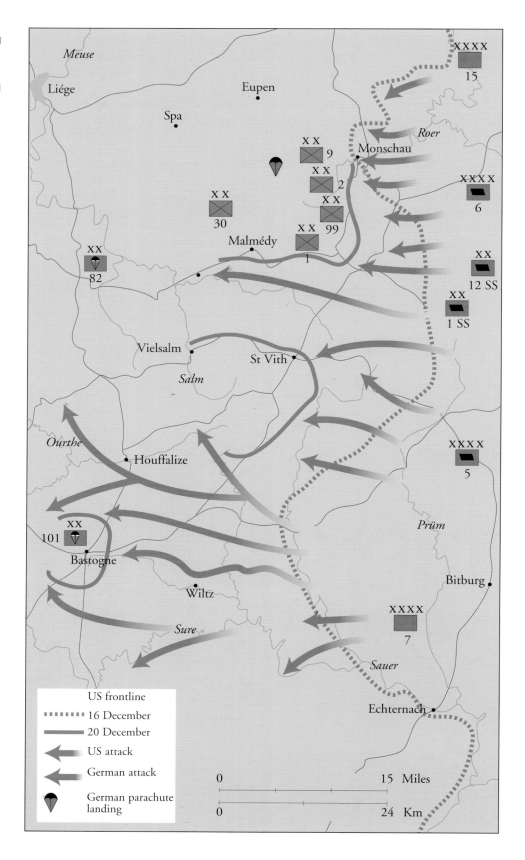

US frontline

.......... 16 December

———— 20 December

◄— US attack

◄— German attack

German parachute landing

0          15   Miles

0          24   Km

by sullen American prisoners. The Germans turned north towards the town of Malmédy.

When the lead Panzer IVs approached a crossroads in the hamlet of Baugnez they spotted a column of US soft-skinned vehicles ahead of them. They immediately started firing on the Americans, then raced at full speed towards them. Panzergrenadiers in armoured halftracks were close behind. Outgunned, the Americans offered no resistance and, in a few minutes, Waffen-SS men had herded almost 100 stunned Americans into a nearby field. Peiper then passed by in his armoured command halftrack and ordered the advance to continue, racing off westwards with his lead tanks. Learning that a US artillery brigade had its headquarters nearby, Peiper set off to capture it and its general. The American general escaped with a few minutes to spare before Peiper's tanks burst into his compound. Back at Baugnez, the captured Americans were being

machine-gunned by Peiper's men in an incident that would become notorious as the "Malmédy Massacre", even though it occurred several kilometres outside the town. Peiper and more than 70 other members of the *Leibstandarte* would later face war crimes charges for their involvement in this horrific incident.

## Stopping at Stavelot

Peiper continued to drive his men forward. They kept going even after it grew dark. The Waffen-SS column was unopposed until it approached the village of Stavelot, where the lead panzers were fired upon by a single bazooka rocket. Fearing a tank ambush in the night, the Kampfgruppe pulled back to wait for daylight, not knowing that the village and its strategic bridge was held by only a few dozen Americans.

Behind Jochen Peiper's spearhead, the *Leibstandarte*'s other Kampfgruppe, led by

■ *Below:* A Waffen-SS panzergrenadier looks over the remnants of an abandoned US column in the Ardennes.

SS-Standartenführer Max Hansen, had already managed to break free and was advancing westwards. Containing the bulk of a panzer-grenadier regiment and most of the division's Panzerjäger IVs, it was operating slightly to the south of Peiper on a parallel Rollbahn.

### The Eisenborn ridge

The *Hitlerjugend* Division was not faring so well in its attempt to open up the northern Rollbahn and seize the strategic Eisenborn ridge. The US 99th Infantry Division put up stiff resistance and held the attacks by the 326th Volksgrenadier Division. Rather than being used to exploit a breach in the American line, the division's two lead Kampfgruppen had to be committed to the assault action. Although the Waffen-SS

Panthers inflicted heavy losses on the few American tanks barring their way, soon GIs with bazookas were picking off the German tanks at an alarming rate. This fierce fighting in a string of border villages allowed time for the Americans to form a firing line with their Shermans, M10 and M18 tank destroyers, and 105mm howitzers in the antitank role.

When the *Hitlerjugend*'s Panthers rolled forward on the morning of 18 December, they ran into a hail of well-aimed antitank fire. They made it to the American lines but soon 15 Panthers, 1 Panzer IV and 2 Panzerjäger IVs were ablaze. A retreat was ordered before more of the *Hitlerjugend*'s valuable armour was lost. Kraas and Dietrich ordered a rethink, and the division's Schwerpunkt was now shifted south in order

■ *Below:* The surrounded defenders of Bastogne had to rely on parachute drops to keep fighting until George Patton's armour broke through on 26 December 1944.

■ *Left:* Bastogne
– the focus for the
American defence
of the southern
sector of the
Ardennes.

to try to bypass the strong defence on Eisenborn ridge. More fanatical American resistance was encountered, and the division spent four days trying to batter its way through. Dietrich concentrated four corps artillery regiments to support a large attack on 21 December, but the Americans were fighting stubbornly and were not to be moved. When the panzer regiment attacked, it lost 11 more tanks. A further attack on the following day met a similar fate, and the division was pulled out of the line to be re-assigned to push through behind the *Leibstandarte* Division.

### The last push for victory

The stalling of the *Hitlerjugend*'s attacks on the morning of 18 December meant that Peiper's Kampfgruppe was now I SS Panzer Corps' Schwerpunkt. Even so, he was still 30km (18.6 miles) from the Meuse and 48 hours behind schedule. This was not a time to worry about his flanks. Peiper pushed all his tanks forward for one last, desperate lunge for victory.

At dawn that day, Peiper renewed his attack with added vigour. The Panthers rolled at full speed into Stavelot to seize its key bridge. The now reinforced defenders knocked

*At dawn Peiper renewed his attack. Panthers rolled at full speed into Stavelot to seize its key bridge*

out the lead Panther, and Peiper – along with the lead panzergrenadiers – took cover at the edge of the village.

Grabbing a Panzerfaust, Peiper set off to take out the offending antitank gun. Another Panther arrived and destroyed the 76mm antitank gun before driving over the bridge in a hail of bullets and shells. Their position unhinged, the Americans now withdrew to safety. This action left Peiper now in control of the vital bridge.

With time critical, Peiper pressed on to seize his next objectives, the bridge over the River Amblève at Trois Ponts, and another bridge slightly farther south across the River Salm. The bulk of the Kampfgruppe headed for Trois Ponts and a small contingent was sent to the Salm. American engineers were hard at work in Trois Ponts, laying demolition charges on the key bridge and mines on

the roads as Peiper's lead Panthers rolled into town just before 11:00 hours.

A well-placed antitank gun immobilized the lead tank and, as the following Waffen-SS tank manoeuvred around the wreckage, the GIs pressed the plunger on their demolition charges. The vital bridge disappeared in a massive mushroom cloud. The same thing happened to the assault team sent to capture the Salm bridge, leaving Peiper's route on the main road westwards blocked. He therefore turned his troops around, and sent them northwards on a side road, which led through the village of La Gleize, in order to bypass the downed bridges.

Two hours later, his Panthers were through the village and heading westwards to the crossing at Cheneux. It was undefended and Peiper's tanks were soon across and heading westwards again. Allied fighter-bombers now swooped down, knocking out two Panthers and a dozen vehicles. The damage inflicted was minor, but the delay proved fatal to Operation Autumn Mist. It gave a group of American engineers just the time they needed to plant demolition charges on Peiper's next target, the bridge at Habiemont. As his Panthers arrived at the bridge at 16.45 hours, the structure was blown in front of Peiper's eyes. Twice in one day his ambitions had been thwarted. He now had to turn his column around and head back to La Gleize to rethink his options. He had only 31 operational tanks: 6 Tigers, 6 Panzer IVs and 19 Panthers. Once back there, he met up with Gustav Knittel's reconnaissance battalion which had now made its way forward, along with a small convoy of fuel tankers. News also came in that American troops had recaptured Stavelot, so Knittel was ordered to retrace his steps and open up a supply route for Peiper.

After a night spent refuelling and reorganizing his tired troops, Peiper launched them into the attack again the following morning. This time he headed northwest towards Stoumont. The first elements of a US blocking force had moved into place in the village during the night, and when his tanks

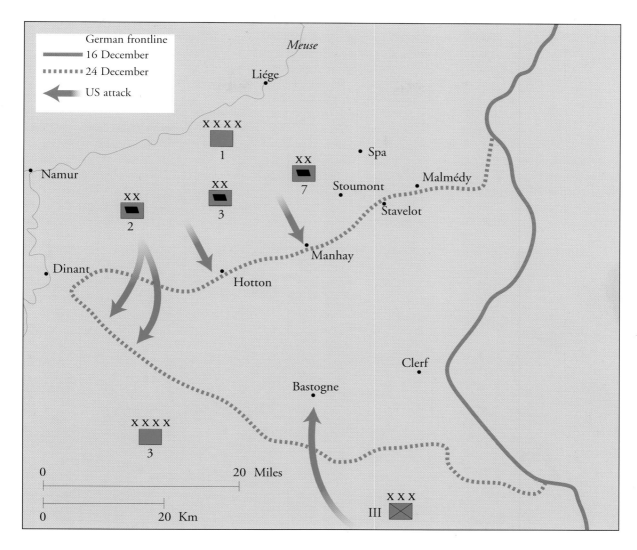

German frontline
16 December
24 December
US attack

Meuse

Liége

Namur

XXXX
1

XX
7

• Spa

XX
3

• Stoumont

Malmédy

XX
2

Stavelot

• Dinant

Manhay

Hotton

• Clerf

• Bastogne

XXXX
3

0          20 Miles

0          20 Km

XXX
III

advanced, they were met by 90mm antitank gunfire. One King Tiger and four Panzer IVs were hit before German infantry cleared the village. When the advance continued, the panzers ran into a battalion of Shermans emerging out of the afternoon gloom. His route blocked, Peiper ordered the panzers back to La Gleize. With American columns closing in from four sides, Peiper was effectively trapped. He held out until the evening of 23 December, when he was given permission to break out. The details of this episode are recounted in the introduction of this book. The majority of his troops were left dead or wounded on the battlefield, along with more then 25 tanks, 50 armoured halftracks and other vehicles. Peiper's lunge for victory had failed.

The remainder of the *Leibstandarte* Division, led by Kampfgruppe *Hansen*, was making desperate efforts to catch up with Peiper, and this soon turned into a rescue mission when the commander of the division's panzer regiment found himself cut off by American reinforcements.

## Stalled until morning

Hansen's advance had at first gone well, brushing aside a column of US reconnaissance troops near Recht on 18 December. Then it was ordered to push northwards towards Stavelot, but traffic chaos in the village prevented it moving until the morning of 19 December. Ten Tigers and Panzer IVs moved in on the village from the south, but their attack was literally stopped in its tracks

■ *Above:* By Christmas 1944, the German attack in the Ardennes had run out of steam – then the Americans counterattacked.

when an American M-10 tank destroyer hit the lead King Tiger's side armour, penetrating the monster panzer and causing it to explode. Access to the bridge was blocked. Knittel's reconnaissance unit mounted its own attack on Stavelot from the west on that day, backed by two of Peiper's King Tigers. His men reached the centre of the village but they were too late to stop American engineers blowing the bridge.

The following day, Hansen's panzergrenadiers renewed their attack on Stavelot but they now were ordered to bypass the village from the south and use forest tracks to find a route through to Peiper. The fighting in the village was some of the fiercest of the whole Ardennes campaign and a number of civilians were killed. Later, *Leibstandarte* men would stand trial for their deaths.

### Hansen by the Salm

The move westwards was more successful and soon Hansen had troops situated overlooking the Salm River. US paratroopers from the 82nd Airborne Division had now arrived in strength, and were starting to build up a strong line blocking the route through to Peiper. The rescue effort eventu-

■ *Below:* German troops loot the boots of dead GIs in a wintry Ardennes village.

■ *Left:* Heavy winter snow turned the poor Ardennes road network into a nightmare, delaying German tank movements.

ally proved futile, and all Hansen's men could do was hold open a bridgehead to receive their beleaguered colleagues. By the time Peiper's men had reached safety on Christmas Day, the *Leibstandarte* Division had shot its bolt. The destruction of Peiper's Kampfgruppe had ripped the heart out of its offensive power. It would be three days before it was able to take the offensive again.

Skorzeny's 150th Panzer Brigade fared little better than the other elements of I SS Panzer Corps. Only a handful of its sabotage teams were able to penetrate American lines, and none of them managed to seize the vital Meuse bridges. The psychological effect of their presence on the battlefield was far more important than their actual achievements. Indeed, they have entered popular legend after their exploits were immortalized in the Hollywood movie "The Battle of the Bulge". In the end, Otto Skorzeny's brigade was committed to a half-hearted frontal assault against Malmédy that was easily repulsed, giving the Americans time to destroy the town's vital bridges.

## Committing II SS Panzer Corps

Four days into Operation Autumn Mist, it was becoming clear that I SS Panzer Corps was stalled. Peiper's Kampfgruppe was stuck at La Gleize and the *Hitlerjugend* was getting nowhere on the Eisenborn ridge. It was time to commit Bittrich's II SS Panzer Corps to action. The rapid advance of Peiper created one opportunity for Dietrich. The US 7th Armored Division and parts of three other divisions were still holding out in the town of St Vith, and were preventing the Germans from securing its vital road junctions. Bittrich's mission was to push his two panzer divisions to the north and south of the St Vith salient, trapping the American force, before pushing westwards to the Meuse. It looked good on a map, but *Das Reich* and *Hohenstaufen*'s Kampfgruppen had to contend with a road network that was hopelessly overloaded. Roads were already congested with units moving to the front, supply columns and the charred remains of US vehicles. Bittrich's Blitzkrieg soon bogged down.

The *Hohenstaufen* Division led the northern pincer, pushing through Recht to attempt to seize Vielsalm. They were hoping to block this area, as it was the main escape route for American troops trapped in St Vith. SS-Sturmbannführer Eberhard Telkamp led the *Hohenstaufen*'s panzer regiment into action on 21 December, and it soon ran into a strong 7th Armored Division Combat Command, with almost 80 Shermans and tank destroyers.

## Christmas carnage

Telkamp had a Panther shot out from under him in his first clash with the Americans. Over the next two days, *Hohenstaufen* troops pressed forward time and again, only to be rebuffed. The battle came to a climax on Christmas Eve, when Telkamp ordered an all-out effort to break through to Vielsalm. Just as his panzer regiment was forming up to attack, USAAF P-47 Thunderbolt fighter-bombers swooped down in waves and massacred his column. Now the *Hohenstaufen*'s northern pincer was well and truly blocked.

*Das Reich* had been ordered south of St Vith, but its column was soon halted when the division's tankers were unable to get past road congestion and deliver the vital fuel to the vehicles. The commander of the reconnaissance battalion of *Das Reich*, SS-Sturmbannführer Ernst-August Krag, was allocated the bulk of his division's scarce fuel on 21 December for the vital task of infiltrating behind the St Vith salient to close the American escape route. The prize was to be the entrapment of 20,000 American troops. Krag's reconnaissance troopers were reinforced with a company of Panzerjäger IVs and a battalion of Wespe 105mm self-propelled guns.

■ *Left:* Once the Allies had held the German advance into the Ardennes, Waffen-SS units had quickly to form defensive lines. Here, a StuG III and 88mm Flak gun defend a road.

■ *Above:* With fuel supplies running short, large quantities of German armour and equipment had to be abandoned in the final days of the offensive.

Using back roads and tracks, Krag managed to slip through the American lines and by the evening of 23 December, he was in the village of Salmchâteau, only 3km (1.8 miles) from Vielsalm. Tanks of the 7th Armored Division were still holding the northern escape route open through that town, but Krag's appearance effectively blocked the southern route out of St Vith. His Kampfgruppe caught the last convoy out of St Vith to use this route.

In a confused night-time ambush, Krag's Panzerjägers quickly shot up the Americans' M5 light tanks, then his artillery started to rake the escaping convoy. The destruction of the American convoy was complete when Panther tanks of the army's Führer Begleit Brigade attacked it from the south. The remainder of the trapped American force had chosen to use the northern route and managed to get through to Vielsalm by

> *In a confused night-time ambush, Krag's Panzerjägers quickly shot up the Americans' M5 light tanks*

19:00 hours, and then the rearguard blew up the town's bridges.

Denied his prize at St Vith, Bittrich was now determined to push *Das Reich* forward to exploit a gap in the American defences at Manhay, which offered a route westwards to the Meuse. SS-Obersturmbannführer Otto Weidinger's *Der Führer* Panzergrenadier Regiment at last received fuel on 22 December and was launched forward with a company of Panzer IVs and StuG IIIs in the lead. It ran into a battalion-sized force of 82nd Airborne paratroopers, artillery batteries, and a platoon of Sherman tanks during the early hours of 23 December at the key Barque de Fraiture crossroads.

When the initial attack was repulsed by the Americans, Weidinger pulled back and brought up his artillery battery to soften up the defenders who were fighting in the woods around the crossroads. After several

hours spent bombarding the US position, Weidinger launched a two-pronged attack. With Panzer IVs and StuG IIIs leading the way, the Waffen-SS then closed in on the Americans. They were soon almost surrounded, then the German tanks started to pick off the Shermans and 105mm howitzers from long range. The three surviving American tanks pulled out through the last escape route, leaving the 100 paratroopers on their own amid 34 destroyed tanks and vehicles. They were soon being rounded up by the Waffen-SS men. Only 44 managed to escape in the confusion.

## Americans at Manhay

The main road to Manhay was now blocked by an American task force, so an infiltration attack was ordered to bypass its positions along narrow forest tracks westwards. Waffen-SS pioneers spent the day widening the roads to take the division's Panthers, while Lammerding's two panzergrenadier regiments were brought forward in preparation for the assault. Several fuel tankers had

also pushed through the clogged roads, so the *Das Reich* Division was set to launch a divisional-sized assault.

Setting off just after last light, the *Das Reich* columns got to within a few metres of the American positions to the southwest of Manhay when American sentries at last realized that something was wrong and started to issue challenges. At this point, it was too late. German commanders fired volleys of flares to illuminate the battlefield and then the Panthers opened fire. Within minutes, 17 Shermans were ablaze and the outlying defences of Manhay were breached. Hearing firing behind them, the bypassed American task force attempted to intervene, but well-placed Panzerjäger IVs knocked out its lead two Shermans. The task force's commander then ordered his men to take to the woods, every man for himself!

The American defenders of Manhay now realized the danger they were in and a retreat was ordered. At this point, a Waffen-SS Panther that had become lost in the night attack just outside the town took a wrong

■ *Above:* Even the mighty Tiger IIs proved unable to hold back the US advance.

against its flanks and, two days later, *Das Reich* had to give up Manhay or face complete encirclement.

## Triple push

Three Waffen-SS divisions were now in the line, next to each other, along the northern edge of the German salient or bulge in the US front. *Das Reich* had pushed the farthest west, and next to it *Hohenstaufen* had come into line. After being rebuffed at Manhay, Bittrich was now facing two US armoured divisions. The remnants of the *Leibstandarte* were still engaged in fighting the 82nd Airborne Division between Trois Ponts and Stavelot. Fuel shortages, the terrible terrain and horrendous road congestion – coupled with heavy snow and freezing nights – were still preventing Dietrich from concentrating his army's fighting power for a decisive breakthrough. Every day that the German advance was stalled gave the Allies precious time during which to bring up reinforcements and muster their strength for their inevitable counterattack.

By 26 December, the *Hitlerjugend* Division had managed to battle its way through the grid-locked road systems and it was positioned on *Das Reich*'s western flank, ready to kick-start the stalled Sixth Panzer Army offensive. Most of the division's panzers and artillery were still stuck in jams many kilometres to the east, so the main responsibility for the attack happened to fall on the 25th SS Panzergrenadier Regiment – helped by *Das Reich*'s Kampfgruppe *Krag* – by accident rather than design.

The regiment had to attack through a heavily wooded hillside towards the village of Erezee, which was strongly defended by American paratroopers, backed by tanks. It was impossible to get any panzers or armoured halftracks through the terrible terrain, so the only fire-support available were three 75mm antitank guns that had to be manhandled by their crews up the hillside. The only other defence against American tanks were the Panzerfaust rockets carried by every man in the Kampfgruppe.

■ *Above:* **A Waffen-SS man captured by the US 82nd Airborne Division shows the strain of two weeks of constant fighting.**

turn on a forest track and drove into the centre of Manhay. When the Americans at last realized that they had a German tank in their midst, all hell broke loose. The tank's commander, SS-Oberscharführer Ernst Barkmann, ordered his driver to reverse out of the town, as he fired off smoke grenades in order to cover their escape. Gun rounds from the Shermans and machine-gun bullets ricocheted off the Panther's armour as it made a speedy exit.

*When the Americans at last realized that they had a German tank in their midst, all hell broke loose*

This single incident turned what had been a well-organized tactical withdrawal into a rout. Hundreds of Americans were streaming north out of the town, at the same time as the remainder of *Das Reich*'s Panthers appeared from the south. Their appearance completed the American rout, and the equivalent of a brigade of troops was now in full flight.

The following day more American tanks arrived to seal the front around *Das Reich*, backed by 18 battalions of artillery. Ordered to press on westwards, Lammerding's men soon hit a rock-solid defence. Other American tank columns began to press in

Starting out early in the evening, the heavily loaded panzergrenadiers had to march through deep snow. It took them five hours to close on their objectives. One battalion stormed into the village of Sadzot, completely surprising its American defenders there, many of whom were trying to keep warm in farmhouses rather than stand outside on sentry duty. The panzergrenadiers soon cleared the village and took many of the defenders prisoner. Surprise was not complete, though, and the Americans managed to get off a radio message calling for help before their command post was overrun. Another panzergrenadier unit pushed on past Sadzot and moved towards Erezee.

## The lost village

Kampfgruppe *Krag* had tried to advance along the main road to Erezee, via the village of Amonines. It ran into a strong road-block and lost a number of armoured vehicles in the dark, so its commander decided that it should turn back.

The Americans now launched their reserve battalion to retake the lost village. They were backed by several M5 Stuart tanks, and for several hours the US paratroopers and Waffen-SS men fought it out in the streets and houses of Sadzot. By dawn 40 dead Germans were left in the village and the panzergrenadier battalion had pulled back to the woods on its outskirts.

The 75mm antitank guns were now duelling with the American tanks, but the heavy US artillery support kept the Germans pinned down. A stalemate reigned throughout the day, during which the *Hitler-jugend* began preparations to push forward again during the course of the coming night.

After leaving behind their vehicles, Kampfgruppe *Krag* was to push forward through the forests to the south of Sadzot, leading two battalions of the 26th SS Panzergrenadier Regiment that had moved up into the line earlier in the day. Their advance was unopposed until they reached the far side of the forest, when heavy American small-arms fire stalled the attack.

A counterattack against the 25th Regiment was rebuffed and incurred heavy losses during the morning of 29 December. Those losses included the destruction of five Stuart light tanks. In terms of manpower during these clashes, more than 120 US paratroopers were lost, either killed or wounded. But such small successes were of little use.

The German High Command ordered the *Hitlerjugend* Division to halt its offensive operations during the afternoon and the division was instructed to pull back. This was not so that it could rest and recuperate: it was now to concentrate for a new offensive elsewhere in the Ardennes.

This was the high water mark of the Waffen-SS advance on the northern wing during Operation Autumn Mist. The tide had now turned irrevocably in favour of the Americans. Adolf Hitler's massive gamble in the West had failed miserably.

The fighting in the Ardennes, however, was far from over. For three more long weeks, the Waffen-SS panzer divisions would find that they were going to have many more bitter battles to fight.

> *The tide had now turned irrevocably in favour of the Americans. Hitler's massive gamble had failed*

■ *Above:* Captured members of Skorzeny's undercover unit were executed by US firing squads for wearing GI uniforms during the Ardennes Offensive.

# CHAPTER 15

# DEATH RIDE

## The aftermath of the Ardennes Offensive in the West.

**A** week after the start of Operation Autumn Mist, the German offensive had well and truly run out of steam. Dietrich's Sixth Panzer Army had been held in check along the Amblève River. To the south, the Fifth Panzer Army had advanced to within 15km (9.3 miles) of the Meuse at Dinant before being turned back by British tanks and Allied fighter-bombers. General of Panzer Troops Hasso von Manteuffel had managed to surround the American 101st Airborne Division in the town of Bastogne. However, a relief column from Lieutenant-General George Patton's Third Army punched through from Luxembourg to lift the siege on 26 December 1944.

With huge Allied reinforcements now pouring in to counter their penetration, German commanders were convinced that the offensive stood no chance of success. They wanted to pull out the surviving panzer divisions and concentrate them as a counterattack force to help prop up the now threatened Eastern Front. Hitler would have none of this. He wanted a renewed offensive to defeat the Americans, by cutting off Bastogne again to open a new route for further westward offensives.

I SS Panzer Corps was to be sent south to close off the narrow 1km- (0.6-mile-) wide corridor linking Bastogne to Patton's army. Again the fuel shortages and poor road conditions meant the Waffen-SS panzer divisions took far too long to get into position to attack. The *Leibstandarte* did not reach its jumping-off position until late on 28 December, and was not ready to attack until late the following

■ *Left:* Good weather in the last week of December 1944 meant Allied airpower pounded Waffen-SS panzer columns in the Ardennes.

day. It arrived ahead of the rest of I SS Panzer Corps, and was sent into action under the command of an army panzer corps.

The division was much reduced in combat power after its heavy losses over the previous 10 days, mustering at the most 50 tanks, including 16 Panthers, 25 Panzer IVs and perhaps 15 King Tigers, as well as 18 Panzerjäger IVs. SS-Sturmbannführer Werner Poetsche now commanded the division's panzers in the absence of Jochen Peiper, who had been evacuated back to Germany after suffering a breakdown following his dramatic escape from La Gleize. His Kampfgruppe was augmented by remnants

■ *Below:* A *Hitlerjugend* **Panther that was knocked out during the fighting around Bastogne.**

of two panzergrenadier battalions. Not all the division's tanks, particularly the King Tigers, were present at the start of its attack.

Max Hansen's Kampfgruppe contained the remainder of the division's infantry and its Panzerjäger IVs. Much of the division's artillery and Nebelwerfers were massed to support the attack, but they were unable to stockpile very much ammunition.

The *Leibstandarte's* westward attack was planned to coincide with an eastward push by the 3rd Panzergrenadier Division and Führer Begleit Brigade, to cut the Bastogne corridor. First to attack were some 30 of Poetsche's panzers, striking out just before

dawn on 30 December. They headed out through morning gloom and, helped by panzergrenadiers, easily cleared out two frontline villages. American tank destroyers then made an appearance, hitting several of the panzers.

As the panzers approached the main road south out of Bastogne across open fields, the Americans mobilized two companies of Shermans to block their path. Now the clouds cleared to allow the intervention of Allied fighter-bombers. For more than two hours, the Thunderbolts worked over the panzer column, claiming seven kills and delaying the advance as the tanks took cover in woods. The American tanks had now taken up ambush positions ahead of the panzers, and were waiting when Poetsche at last got his forces moving again.

Poetsche's command Panther was knocked out by the first American shot, and soon nine panzers were blazing. The panzergrenadiers had to go to ground until they could pull back as it got dark.

To the south, Kampfgruppe *Hansen* was led by seven Panzerjäger IVs through the

## Poetsche's Panther was knocked out by the first American shot, and soon nine panzers were blazing

heavy woods surrounding the village of Villers-la-Bonne-Eau at dawn. The Waffen-SS men soon surrounded the defenders in the small village and spent the rest of the morning clearing them out. Early in the afternoon, the advance was pressed forward and, in a few hours, they were through the woods on the edge of the main road south out of Bastogne. Reinforcements were pushed in at nightfall and the *Leibstandarte* tried to secure its positions overnight. The news that the eastward attack by their army colleagues had failed did little to raise the Waffen-SS men's sagging morale.

For the next week the *Leibstandarte* soldiers held their hard-won ground against a series of strong US counterattacks, backed by tanks and large quantities of artillery. The Waffen-SS panzers found themselves "firefighting" small local incursions by American tanks on the fringes of the positions held by the panzergrenadiers. Two precious King Tigers and several other panzers were lost in these scattered battles.

As the *Leibstandarte* was being brought to a halt south of Bastogne, I SS Panzer

Corps was being mustered to the north of the town for a final push for victory. *Hitlerjugend* and *Hohenstaufen* had been pulled out of the northern shoulder and sent south, along with the 340th Volksgrenadier Division. Field Marshal Model visited the corps headquarters north of Bastogne on 2 January 1945 in order to put his seal of approval on the plans to smash open the American defences the following day. *Hohenstaufen* was to drive in from northwest of the town and *Hitlerjugend* would attack from the northeast, as the Volksgrenadiers linked them together. Several Volks artillery brigades were mustered to provide fire support, which was fortunate, because the *Hitlerjugend*'s guns were stranded to the north due to lack of fuel.

The Americans, however, were quicker off the draw and put in an attack against the Volksgrenadiers during the afternoon of 2 January. As the Americans reached the outskirts of Bourcy, the advanced Kampfgruppe of the *Hitlerjugend*'s panzer regiment was just driving through the village from the north. Eleven Panthers and Panzer IVs immediately engaged the advance guard of the American column, sending it reeling back to its start-line.

At 09:00 hours on 3 January, the German attack was launched as planned. Led by 20 Panzer IVs, the *Hohenstaufen* advanced in the face of heavy American anti-tank fire. The attack stalled in the afternoon when the panzers were caught in open ground. Another attack was attempted in the early evening and suffered a similar fate. The division tried a surprise raid later in the night and penetrated some distance behind American lines before it was beaten back.

## On to Bastogne

In the early afternoon the Volksgrenadiers and *Hitlerjugend* began to move forward. The Volksgrenadiers were soon bogged down in heavy fighting in large forests. *Hitlerjugend*'s panzer regiment led the division forward along the open ground to the left of the railway track, which headed south into the centre of Bastogne. It put 13 Panzer IVs, 7 Panthers and 15 Panzerjäger IVs into action, along with 28 Jagdpanzer IVs and 13 Jagdpanthers of the attached 560th Anti-

Tank Battalion. Panzergrenadiers in armoured halftracks were close behind the German armour, and during the afternoon the armada made steady progress, advancing 3km (1.8 miles) despite heavy American artillery fire.

In a night attack, the *Hitlerjugend* made a further big advance, reaching the edges of the villages of Magaret and Bizory on the northern outskirts of Bastogne. Panzergrenadiers and Panzerjäger IVs now pressed into the large Azette wood in front of the town, cutting to pieces a US infantry battalion.

More attacks were now launched against Magaret and Bizory in the afternoon by the panzer regiment, but they couldn't dislodge the defenders. Wild rumours of German

breakthroughs caused panic and some GIs fled into Bastogne. Panzers penetrated the villages, only to be driven back by American Shermans and bazooka teams. The line held.

## Panzer push on Hill 510

Over on the northwestern edge of the American line, the *Hohenstaufen* panzers were again pushing forward, making local gains as well as overruning a number of trench lines.

During the afternoon of 5 January the *Hitlerjugend* panzers made one last lunge to capture Hill 510 outside Magaret, which overlooked Bastogne. Heavy American tank- and artillery fire soon forced the Germans to pull back from the exposed position. This wall of fire was instrumental in blunting the Waffen-SS attack, making it impossible for the *Hitlerjugend* men to even contemplate further movement towards Bastogne.

An American breakthrough against the northern shoulder of the German front forced the withdrawal of the *Hohenstaufen* from Bastogne on 6 January. The *Hitlerjugend* Division was now totally exhausted by its exertions and had to spend the next two days consolidating its hard-won gains. Plans were already in hand to pull the division out of the line when it was called upon to make one last drive to capture Hill 510. Under the concentrated fire of all the division's artillery and tanks, its panzer-grenadiers reached the summit of the hill by

■ *Below:* **After regaining their composure, the Allies began to pour troops in to crush the German "bulge" into the Ardennes.**

■ *Right:* British armour joined the Allied counterstroke, helping to strike into the northern flank of the German forces in the Ardennes.

mid-morning on 8 January. Yet again, the Americans massed their artillery fire, which swept the hillside and forced the Waffen-SS men to fall back by midday, leaving 50 dead behind.

On 9 January, Hitler finally realized that trying to take Bastogne was a lost cause and authorized the withdrawal of the Waffen-SS divisions. The *Leibstandarte* was at last able to pull out of its exposed salient into the Bastogne corridor, after Patton launched an attack farther to the east aimed at cutting the division's escape route. The order to withdraw had come just in time, and the last *Leibstandarte* convoys were engaged by American tanks as they made their way eastwards, suffering heavy losses. Artillery and air strikes later joined in to pound the *Leibstandarte* as it made its escape.

While I SS Panzer Corps was gathering around St Vith, II SS Panzer Corps found itself locked in a bitter battle with US armour advancing southwards. *Das Reich* bore the brunt of the defensive fighting until the *Hohenstaufen* could join the fray. They steadily fell back until orders were issued on 16 January for them to be taken out of the line to join their sister Waffen-SS divisions in Army Group B's reserve. Fuel shortages and the chaos meant this was not actually achieved for several days. Hitler then ordered the four Waffen-SS divisions and Dietrich's headquarters to be withdrawn from the Western Front to be refitted for operations on the Eastern Front, where a new Russian offensive was underway.

Operation Autumn Mist was officially over. Hitler's gamble had failed. The Germans lost 33,000 dead, 22,500 missing and 34,000 wounded. They also left behind more than 600 smashed tanks in the Ardennes. The Americans lost 8600 dead, 21,000 missing and 30,000 wounded, along with more than 733 destroyed tanks.

The Waffen-SS had spearheaded the operation and made some of the deepest penetrations into American lines. Many senior Waffen-SS officers, such as Dietrich, had been sceptical about its chances of success, but had given it their best shot. No one could accuse them of not trying, but no amount of bravery and tactical flare could make up for the fact that Hitler's plan was too ambitious and the US Army too powerful.

> *The Americans massed their artillery fire, which swept the hillside and forced the Waffen-SS to fall back*

Figures for losses in the Waffen-SS divisions are hard to come by. Dietrich's Sixth Panzer Army lost some 10,000 dead in total. The armoured vehicle strength of the Waffen-SS divisions was soon restored to near establishment thanks to the smooth recovery of wrecked and damaged tanks from the early phases of the battle. Harder to replace were officer and noncommissioned officer casualties that ran to nearly 50 percent in some Waffen-SS units.

## Operation Solstice

The departure of Dietrich's Sixth Panzer Army – which was soon to be renamed the Sixth SS Panzer Army – did not mark the end of the participation of Waffen-SS panzer divisions against the Western Allies.

In tandem with his plan to strike into the Ardennes, Hitler had long dreamed of pushing into Alsace and retaking the border city of Strasbourg. Army Group G was to strike south in Operation North Wind, with the 17th SS Panzergrenadier Division in the lead, in order to outflank the city. The division was rebuilt after being heavily battered around Metz in November 1944 and bolstered with the delivery of 57 StuG IIIs in early December. When the attack began on New Year's Eve, the Waffen-SS division achieved the deepest penetration of the American lines until strong counter-attacks halted it. Three days of heavy fighting followed in which the division's commander, SS-Standartenführer Hans Linger, was captured when he took a wrong turn near the frontline as he drove in his command Volkswagen.

Hitler now launched Operation Solstice. Its aim was to drive a pincer around Strasbourg from the south and it was to be conducted under the command of Army Group Upper Rhine. The refitted *Frundsberg* Division was committed to this offensive on 13 January 1945, and its 36 Panzer IVs and 35 Panthers made good progress until the operation ran out of steam a week later. In a final irony, the veteran Waffen-SS general, Paul Hausser, who had recovered from his injuries received in Normandy, was placed in command of Army Group Upper Rhine for what would be the final months of the war from 29 January.

Soon the needs of the Eastern Front also resulted in Hausser losing the *Frundsberg* Division. The 17th SS Division was the only Waffen-SS armoured unit to remain on the Western Front until the end of the war. By 25 March, it had been reduced to some 800 men who were desperately holding the last German bridgehead on the west bank of the Rhine. The *Frundsberg* managed to escape across the mighty river, but the Americans caught up with the division at Nuremberg, where it tried to mount a series of rearguard actions during early April. It then surrendered to the Americans.

■ *Left:* In the wake of the German retreat was total devastation.

# CHAPTER 16

# LAST ACTIONS

## The end of the war and the legacy of the Waffen-SS.

In the final days of January 1945, "Sepp" Dietrich's battered panzer divisions went through one last cycle of receiving new equipment and recruits to prepare them for another offensive. This time their Führer wanted his panzer élite to turn back the Soviet spearheads that had overrun Hungary and were threatening the Third Reich's last oilfields.

The Waffen-SS veterans of the *Leibstandarte*, *Das Reich*, *Hohenstaufen* and *Hitlerjugend* Divisions went through the procedures of preparing for this new battle, but many were just going through the motions and were openly talking about Germany losing the war. Others were dismayed that Hitler was even contemplating sending his last armoured reserves on a wild-goose chase into a backwater, when the might of the Red Army was less than 80km (50 miles) from Berlin itself.

The Führer wanted his offensive, and he got it. In mid-February, Dietrich's troopers launched forward into their final offensive, going into battle alongside their Waffen-SS comrades from the *Wiking* and *Totenkopf* Divisions. Dietrich's army was renamed the Sixth SS Panzer Army to signify its enhanced status. For a month they seemed to have the initiative, bringing back memories of the old days. It was not to last. The Soviets soon regained their composure, then began to drive back the Waffen-SS men. Gaining momentum, the Soviet steamroller started to roll westwards. Dietrich's men barely managed to get out of Hungary, and were struggling to avoid encirclement.

■ *Left:* In the first months of 1945 the remnants of the Wehrmacht were pounded from the air and on the ground by the Allies.

Hitler was furious that his favoured Waffen-SS divisions had ignored his orders to fight to the last man. Underground in his Berlin bunker with Soviet troops closing in, a ranting Hitler insisted that the *Leibstandarte* and *Hitlerjugend* men remove his name from their sleeve cuffs. This was the final straw for the dispirited men of Dietrich's battered army as they struggled across the Austrian border. Dietrich's remaining troops tried to stage a rearguard action to defend Vienna, but it was futile. Soon they were heading westwards again. Once

> *Hitler was furious his Waffen-SS divisions had ignored his orders to fight to the last man*

back on German soil, many of the conscripts now serving in the ranks of the Waffen-SS began to drift away. The hardcore officers started to concentrate on getting themselves and their remaining men away from the vengeful Soviets. Fighting the Führer's war was no longer their priority.

### Rush for safety

When Hitler committed suicide in Berlin on 29 April, he released his Praetorian Guard of their oath of loyalty to him. The retreat through Austria and Czechoslovakia now became a headlong rush for the West and safety. It was hoped the British and Americans would afford them civilized treatment as prisoners of war under the terms of the Geneva Convention.

In the first week of May 1945, as Germany formally surrendered, the Waffen-SS panzer divisions entered captivity in different degrees of dignity. The bulk of Dietrich's army managed to escape the Soviet armoured columns which were snapping at their heels. When the hour came for them to lay down their arms, many of the Waffen-SS men meekly surrendered to American troops. Others took to the hills in the hope of finding their way home. Dietrich himself headed for Switzerland, dressed in traditional Bavarian costume, with his wife. Many of these fugitives, including Dietrich, were captured, although some were spirited away by the shadowy Odessa group to exile in Switzerland, Spain and South America. *Das Reich*'s Heinz Lammerding and the flamboyant Otto Skorzeny were among the lucky few.

The *Leibstandarte*, *Das Reich* and *Wiking* Divisions managed to evade Czech partisans to reach American lines, then just melted into the countryside and never formally surrendered. The *Hitlerjugend* Division marched up to American lines to surrender, but when a Soviet tank column appeared, its men panicked and stampeded straight past the GIs. The *Hohenstaufen* Division was able to peacefully surrender en masse to American troops, but its sister *Frundsberg* Division from II SS Panzer Corps was fighting in Czechoslovakia at the end of the war and was overrun. Most of its men ended up in Stalin's Siberian Gulag. A similar fate awaited the men of the *Totenkopf* Division which, although it managed to surrender to the Americans, was handed over to the Soviets.

As the remnants of Dietrich's army were being rounded up in a string of temporary prisoner-of-war camps spread through southern Germany, it began to dawn on the Waffen-SS that the victorious Western Allies were not going to treat them as honourable defeated opponents. The officers were soon separated from their men, and squads of investigators arrived to take statements about the deaths of Allied prisoners of war in a spate of incidents from Normandy to the Ardennes.

At the Nuremburg War Crimes Trials, the Allies declared that the whole of the SS, including the Waffen-SS, was a criminal organization. At a stroke, the imprisoned Waffen-SS men were stripped of the protection of the Geneva Convention. Soon the war crimes trials started. The Canadians went after Kurt Meyer and his *Hitlerjugend* men for their alleged involvement in the killing of their captured soldiers in the battles after D-Day. *Das Reich* commanders were pursued by the French for the Oradour massacre, and Lammerding was condemned to death in absentia.

Many *Leibstandarte* officers were rounded up by the Americans, herded into the former concentration camp at Dachau, and tried for

■ *Left:* Some elements of the Waffen-SS refused to accept that the war was over, holding field court martials to execute soldiers refusing to fight to the death for the Führer and Fatherland.

■ *Right:* The *Hitlerjugend* Division was among the finest fighting formations in Hitler's army.

the killings of captured GIs in the Ardennes. The mass trial of the *Leibstandarte* commanders, including Dietrich and Peiper, had a theatrical quality about it. Many of the 74 defendants said they had been tortured into signing confessions, and the trial was rigged against them. Given Dietrich's role in the extra-judicial executions during the early years of Hitler's reign of terror, this was rather ironic. Peiper and 42 others were sentenced to death by hanging. All the others, including Dietrich, either received life sentences or – such as Dietrich's faithful chief of staff, Fritz Kraemer – got similar long spells in prison. The Italians joined the war crimes effort, attempting to get Peiper extradited for the killing of civilians during the *Leibstandarte*'s brief posting to their country in the autumn of 1943. Peiper successfully

resisted this move. Two *Leibstandarte* members, however, were convicted by a Belgian court in 1948 for their part in the killing of civilians in Stavelot.

### British leniency

The British were less inclined to participate in this process. Perhaps the good treatment of the thousands of British paratroopers captured at Arnhem by Bittrich's II SS Panzer Corps meant that the Waffen-SS was less of a hate principle to the British public. The only Waffen-SS commander suspected of killing British POWs, Wilhelm Mohnke, was never prosecuted. He had been captured in Hitler's Berlin bunker by the Russians, and did not return home from Siberia until 1955. He was never charged, and was still living in freedom in Hamburg in the 1990s.

Paul Hausser and Willi Bittrich were held and charged by the British, along with several senior Wehrmacht generals – including the famous Erich von Manstein – of war crimes in German-occupied Russia. They were convicted of being in command appointments when mass murder and other war crimes occurred.

## Commuted sentences for the SS

By the early 1950s, the international mood had changed, as the Western Allies were locked into the Cold War with Stalin's Soviet Union. The western part of Germany was rehabilitated as the Federal Republic and the frontline base for NATO's military stand-off with the Communist Warsaw Pact. Only two *Hitlerjugend* men were ever executed for war crimes. All the rest had their sentences commuted. Slowly and without fanfare, the Waffen-SS men were released from jail. Jochen Peiper was one of the last to be set free in 1957.

The newly released Hausser and Meyer formed HIAG, the Waffen-SS veterans' organization, to campaign to rehabilitate Hitler's

élite fighting unit. They attempted to have the German parliament, the Bundestag, to differentiate between the General-SS and Waffen-SS. It was defeated in 1961.

Most of the former Waffen-SS officers and soldiers tried to put the war behind them and make a living in the new Germany. They shared many different fates. Lammerding, as well as Heinz Harmel and Walther Harzer, all became successful businessmen. Others went on to become minor public officials or lowly labourers.

The infamous Peiper, the so-called butcher of Malmédy, became the lightning rod for the public obsession with all things Nazi. He was hounded from one job to another. The Italian Government tried to have him extradited, then Italian workers in the Volkswagen car factory boycotted him. In 1970 he slipped quietly out of Germany and moved to France to try to live out his remaining years in obscurity, earning a living translating books.

When a French newspaper tracked him down to his log cabin in Traves, he started to receive death threats, allegedly from the

■ *Below:* The Waffen-SS panzer divisions proved themselves to be some of the most effective armoured forces in the history of modern warfare.

Italian Red Brigades terrorist group. On 14 July 1976 his house was attacked by unknown gunmen. The former Waffen-SS commander was killed and his cabin burned to the ground. No one was ever brought to justice for the incident.

More than 50 years after the end of World War II, the exploits of the Waffen-SS continue to be the subject of debate. They are portrayed either as evil war criminals, or as simple soldiers who were on the wrong side of the victors' justice.

### The zealous Waffen-SS

The Allied trials of the Waffen-SS men were far from perfect, but they were more than most Nazi victims ever received. These Waffen-SS men were almost all volunteers and fanatical Nazis. They all believed in the justice of their cause and fought the war with a degree of zeal rarely found on the Allied side. Of the million or so men who served in the Waffen-SS, over one-third died in battle. This was an unprecedented level of casualties that few other fighting formations, outside the Imperial Japanese Army, could equal.

On the battlefields of northwest Europe in the last year of the war, Hitler's Waffen-SS gave their all for him. In Normandy they thwarted all of General Montgomery's attempts to break out of his bridgeheads and, after the American breakout, Waffen-SS generals took charge of the situation, leading trapped German Army units to safety out of the Falaise Kessel.

At Arnhem, the lightning reaction of II SS Panzer Corps put paid to Montgomery's ambitious plan to end the war by Christmas. Two months later the Waffen-SS was in the forefront of the Ardennes Offensive, making some of the deepest penetration into American lines. The fact they got so far, given the terrible weather and road conditions, was a remarkable feat of arms. Even though Hitler's plan was fundamentally flawed and over-ambitious, Waffen-SS commanders gave it their best shot. Five years into the war, despite their over-riding losses, they still believed Germany could win.

*In the Waffen-SS, over one-third died in battle, an unprecedented level of casualties*

In the end, the Waffen-SS troops were unable to turn back the Allied tide. Less than a year after D-Day, Hitler's Thousand Year Reich was in ruins. Their tactical prowess and fanatical fighting spirit could not compensate for Allied numerical and materiel superiority. For every Sherman tank the Waffen-SS knocked out in Normandy, there were 10 to take its place. At the same time, thousands of Allied fighter-bombers swarmed over the German Army in Normandy, denying it the freedom of manoeuvre.

On top of this must be added the effect of the Führer's crazy orders to hold to the last man in every situation. While the fanatical resistance of the Waffen-SS undoubtedly lengthened the war, Hitler's insistence on holding Caen, his mad Mortain counter-attack and his demands that the Ardennes offensive be continued into January 1945, all doomed the Waffen-SS to suffer horrendous and irreplaceable losses. Without the Führer's interference, the Waffen-SS panzers might have held out even longer.

For the opponents of the Waffen-SS panzer divisions, the experience was traumatic. For the British and Canadian armies in Normandy, fighting the Waffen-SS resulted in casualty levels on a par with those experienced in World War I. The British Army ended the war in total awe of its German opponents, and began to recast its armoured doctrine and tactics along the lines of those used by the Waffen-SS in Normandy. The all-arms battle group became the normal tactical formation, and the mission command procedure was adopted instead of the rigid directed command method used in Normandy. The main post-war British tank, the Chieftain, was designed along the lines of the German Tiger. It was designed with armoured protection and firepower as the overriding priority, rather than the vehicle's mobility.

The Americans, who never had to face large numbers of Tigers in Normandy, stuck to their concept of having lightly armoured medium tanks, along the lines of the

Sherman. It was not until the 1970s that the Americans followed the lead of the British, and opted to field a heavily armoured tank, the M1 Abrams. This was part of a major effort by the US Army to recast its doctrine and equipment to counter the Soviets on NATO's central front. Suddenly, the Americans looked to the experiences of the Waffen-SS armoured units in their defensive battles and began to draw lessons from the tactics of their former enemies.

Fortunately for the people of occupied Europe, the attempt by Hitler's Waffen-SS panzer divisions to hold back the Allies failed. In the autumn of 1944 France and Belgium were freed from Nazi tyranny. The defeat of Operation Autumn Mist prevented the return of German rule to Belgium and the final defeat of Germany in May 1945 completed the liberation of Europe.

Hitler's élite panzer force was designed and built to protect his murderous regime. Behind its protective shield, millions of innocents were slaughtered and others oppressed. Evil certainly reigned in the shadow of the Waffen-SS.

■ *Below:* Dachau concentration camp was an appropriate venue for the trial of Waffen-SS war criminals. Hitler's élite troopers were shown to be the guardians of evil.

# SS PANZER DIVISION
## (Total strength: 13–15,000 men)
### Divisional HQ Company (2 x PzKpfw V), band and field police (450 men)

**SS-PANZER REGIMENT** (1600 men)
HQ Company (320 men)

**I Abteilung** (500–600 men)
HQ Company: 2–8 PzKpfw V, 3 x 20mm Flakvierling and 12 x LMG
1, 2, 3 & 4 Companies (each 14–17 PzKpfw V and/or PzKpfw IV)

**II Abteilung** (500 men)
HQ Company, as above but all PzKpfw IV
5 & 6 Companies (each 14 PzKpfw IV)
7 & 8 Companies (each 10–14 75mm Jagdpanzer IV/70)

**I SS-PANZERGRENADIER REGIMENT**
(2000 men)
HQ Company, SdKfz 250 & 251 halftracks (160 men)

**I Abteilung** (all SdKfz 251 halftracks)
(850 men)
HQ Company
1, 2 & 3 Companies (each 2 x 75mm Pak 40, 7 x 20mm Flak 38, 2 x 80mm GrW 34 mortar, 4 x HMG & 29 x LMG)
4 Company (6 x 75mm Pak 40, 4 x 120mm sGrW 42 mortar, 2 x HMG & 4 x LMG)

**II Abteilung** (all truck-mounted) (850 men)
HQ Company
5, 6 & 7 Companies (each 2 x 80mm GrW 34 mortar, 4 x HMG)
8 Company (6 x 20mm Flak 38, 4 x sGrW 42 & 2 x HMG)
(NB: No 9–14 Companies)
15 Company (6 x Hummel, siG 33 or Wespe)
Engineer Company (24 x Flamethrower, 1 x 20mm Flak 38, 2 x 80mm GrW 34, 2 x HMG)

**II SS-PANZERGRENADIER REGIMENT**
As above except both abteilungen as II/I and Engineer Company only 16 x Flammenwerfer and 12 x LMG

**SS-PANZER ARTILLERY REGIMENT** (1600 men)
HQ Company (2 x LMG) (90 men)

**I Abteilung** (550 men)
HQ Company (1 x Wespe, 3 x 20mm Flak 38)
1 & 2 Batteries (each 6 x Wespe)
3 Battery (6 x Hummel)

**II Abteilung** (450 men)
HQ Company (as above)
4 & 5 Batteries (each 6 x towed 105mm leFH 18)

**III Abteilung** (500 men)
HQ Company (as above)
6 & 7 Batteries (each 4 x towed 150mm sFH 18)
8 Battery (4 x 170mm K18)

**SS-PANZER RECONNAISSANCE ABTEILUNG**
(500 men)
HQ Company
Scout Company (26 x SdKfz 221 & 16 x SdKfz 231)
Light Company (SdKfz 251s) (2 x 75mm PaK 40, 2 x 80mm GrW 34 & 44 x LMG)
3 Company (2 x 75mm Pak 40, 7 x 20mm Flak 38, 2 x 80mm GrW 34, 4 x HMG & 29 x LMG)
4 Company (6 x 75mm PaK 40, 6 x 80mm GrW 34, 18 x LMG)
Maintenance Company (5 x LMG)

**SS-PANZERJÄGER ABTEILUNG**
(500 men)
HQ Company (3 x 75mm Jagdpanzer 1V/70)
1 & 2 Companies (each 10 x 75mm Jagdpanzer IV/70)
3 Company (12 x towed 75mm Pak 40)
Maintenance Company (3 x LMG)

**SS-PANZER FLAK ABTEILUNG** (750 men)
HQ Company (2 x LMG)
1 & 2 Companies (each 6 x towed 88mm Flak 18 or 36 & 3 x 20mm Flak 38)
3 Company (9 x 37mm Flak 36 or 37)
4 Company (4–12 x 20mm Flakvierling on halftracks)

**SS-PANZER ENGINEER ABTEILUNG**
(850 men)
HQ Company (4 x LMG & 4 x Flamethrower)
1 Company (motorized) (4 x HMG, 36 x LMG & 4 x 80mm GrW 34)
2 Company (SdKfz 251s) (2 x HMG, 43 x LMG, 2 x 8cm GrW 34 & 6–8 x Flamethrower)

**SS-PANZER SIGNALS ABTEILUNG** (500 men)
HQ Company
3 companies

**SS-PANZER ROCKET ARTILLERY ABTEILUNG**
(500 men)
HQ Company (1 x LMG)
1, 2 & 3 Batteries (each 6 x 150mm WGr 41)
Maintenance Company (1 x LMG)

**SS-MAINTENANCE ABTEILUNG (motorized)**
HQ Company
1, 2, 3, 4 & 5 Transport Companies

# WAFFEN-SS OPERATIONAL PANZER STRENGTH IN NORMANDY, 6 June to 13 August 1944

|  | 1 June | 1 July | 18 July | 25 July | 5 August | 13 August |
|---|---|---|---|---|---|---|
| **Panther tanks** | | | | | | |
| *Leibstandarte* Division | 38 | 25 | 46 | 34 | 46 | 7 |
| *Das Reich* Division | 25 | 26 | unknown | 41 | 1 | 3 |
| *Hohenstaufen* Division | 30 | 19 | 25 | 23 | 11 | 15 |
| *Hitlerjugend* Division | 48 | 24 | 21 | 37 | 9 | 7 |
| **Panzer IV tanks** | | | | | | |
| *Leibstandarte* Division | 42 | 30 | 61 | 45 | 57 | 14 |
| *Das Reich* Division | 44 | 50 | unknown | 37 | 4 | 5 |
| *Hohenstaufen* Division | 41 | 10 | 20 | 21 | 8 | 11 |
| *Frundsberg* Division | 34 | 20 | 12 | 14 | 10 | 11 |
| *Hitlerjugend* Division | 91 | 32 | 16 | 21 | 37 | 17 |
| **StuG III assault guns** | | | | | | |
| *Leibstandarte* Division | 44 | 31 | 35 | 32 | 27 | 8 |
| *Das Reich* Division | 33 | 36 | unknown | 25 | 6 | 8 |
| *Hohenstaufen* Division | 38 | 22 | 15 | 14 | 8 | 14 |
| *Frundsberg* Division | 32 | 25 | 6 | 11 | 7 | 5 |
| 17th SS Division | 42 | 18 | ? | 10 | unknown | unknown |
| **Tiger I tanks** | | | | | | |
| 101st SS Battalion | 37 | 11 | 6 | 13 | 20 | 8 |
| 102nd SS Battalion | 28 | 14 | 19 | 30 | 20 | 7 |
| **Panzerjäger IV** | | | | | | |
| *Hitlerjugend* Division | | | | | 10 | 5 |
| 17th SS Division | | | | | 31 | unknown |

# NORMANDY ORDER OF BATTLE

**PANZER GROUP WEST**
**(then Fifth Panzer Army from 6 August 1944)**
(Date in brackets is when unit reached the Normandy Front)

## I SS Panzer Corps *Leibstandarte Adolf Hitler* (7 June)
(SS-Obergruppenführer Josef "Sepp" Dietrich)
schwer SS-Panzer Abteilung 101: 37 x Tiger I
*SS-Arko I* (artillery command)
*SS-Artillerie Abteilung 101*: 4 x 210mm, 6 x 170mm
*SS-Corps Nachrichten Abteilung 101/501*

## 1st SS Panzer Division *Leibstandarte Adolf Hitler* (25 June to 6 July)
(SS-Brigadeführer Teddy Wisch)
Total strength: 19,618 men
*SS-Panzergrenadier Regiment 1 "LSSAH"*:
I & II Abteilungen only, 36 APC
*SS-Panzergrenadier Regiment 2 "LSSAH"*
*SS-Panzer Regiment "LSSAH"*: 103 x Panzer IV, 72 x Panther
*SS-Sturmgeschütz Abteilung "LSSAH" 1*:
45 x StuG III
*SS-Panzer Artillerie Regiment "LSSAH" 1*:
I & II Abteilungen: 8 x 105mm, 6 x 150mm, 4 x 100mm, 8 x Wespe, 5 x Hummel
*SS-Flak Abteilung "LSSAH" 1*: 12 x 88mm, 9 x 37mm
*SS-Werfer Abteilung "LSSAH" 1*: one battery, 5 x Nebelwerfer
*SS-Panzer Nachrichten Abteilung "LSSAH" 1*
*SS-Panzer Aufklärungs Abteilung "LSSAH" 1*
*SS-Panzer Pionier Abteilung "LSSAH" 1*

## 12th SS Panzer Division *Hitlerjugend* (7 June)
(SS-Oberführer Fritz Witt until 14 June 1944, then SS-Standartenführer Kurt Meyer)
Total strength: 17,000 men, 306 APC
*SS-Panzergrenadier Regiment 25*

*III Abteilung*: 12 x Pak 40, 12 x 75mm IG, 6 x 150mm IG, 2 x 20mm flak
*SS-Panzergrenadier Regiment 26*: 12 x Pak 40, 22 x 75mm IG, 6 x 150mm IG, 2 x 20mm Flak
*SS-Panzer Regiment 12*: 66 x Panther, 98 x Panzer IV
*SS-Panzerjäger Abteilung 12*: one company with 10 x Pzjgr IV
*SS-Panzer Artillerie Regiment 12*: 12 x Wespe, 6 x Hummel, 18 x 105mm, 4 x 150mm, 4 x 100mm
*SS-Flak Abteilung 12*: 12 x 88mm, 9 x 37mm
*SS-Werfer Abteilung 12*: one battery (arrived 12 June, balance in July)
*SS-Panzer Nachrichten Abteilung 12*
*SS-Panzer Aufklärungs Abteilung 12*
*SS-Panzer Pionier Abteilung 12*
*SS-Panzer Ersatz Abteilung 12* (in Arnhem with 2000 men)

## II SS Panzer Corps Headquarters (28 June)
(SS-Obergruppenführer Paul Hausser, then Willi Bittrich from 28 June 1944 )
schwer SS-Panzer Abteilung 102: 28 x Tiger I
*SS-Arko II* (artillery command)
*SS-Corps Nachrichten Abteilung 400*

## 9th SS Panzer Division *Hohenstaufen* (28 June)
(SS-Gruppenführer Willi Bittrich until 28 June 1944, SS-Standartenführer Thomas Müller until 14 July 1944, then SS-Standartenführer Sylvester Stadler)
Total strength: 15,898 men, 345 trucks
*SS-Panzergrenadier Regiment 19*: 9 x Pak 40, 12 x 75mm IG, 6 x 150mm IG, 11 x 20mm Flak
*SS-Panzergrenadier Regiment 20*: 9 x Pak 40, 14 x 75mm IG, 6 x 150mm IG, 12 x 20mm flak
*SS-Panzer Regiment 9*
*I Abteilung*: 79 x Panther
*II Abteilung*: 48 x Panzer IV and 40 x StuG III
*SS-Panzerjäger Abteilung 9*: one company with

12 x Pak 40
*SS-Panzer Artillerie Regiment 9*: 12 x Wespe, 2 x Hummel, 12 x 105m, 12 x 150mm, 4 x 100mm
*SS-Flak Abteilung 9*: 12 x 88mm, 9 x 37mm
*SS-Panzer Nachrichten Abteilung 9*
*SS-Panzer Aufklärungs Abteilung 9*
*SS-Panzer Pionier Abteilung 9*

## 10th SS Panzer Division *Frundsberg* (28 June)
(SS-Oberführer Heinz Harmel)
Total strength: 15,800 men
*SS-Panzergrenadier Regiment 21*
*SS-Panzergrenadier Regiment 22*
*SS-Panzer Regiment 10*: II Abteilung only with 39 x Panzer IV, 38 x StuG III
*SS-Panzer Artillerie Regiment 10*: 11 x Wespe, 6 x Hummel, 12 x 105mm, 12 x 150mm, 4 x 100mm
*SS-Flak Abteilung 10*: 12 x 88mm, 9 x 37mm
*SS-Panzer Nachrichten Abteilung 10*
*SS-Panzer Aufklärungs Abteilung 10*
*SS-Panzer Pionier Abteilung 10*
*SS Ersatz Battalion 9*: 1000 men

## SEVENTH ARMY
## 2nd SS Panzer Division *Das Reich* (1 July)
(SS-Brigadeführer Heinz Lammerding)
Total strength: 227x APC, 768 x trucks, 11,175 men
*SS-Panzergrenadier Regiment 3 Deutschland*: *I & III Abteilung* only
*SS-Panzergrenadier Regiment Der Führer*: *I & III Abteilung* only
*SS-Panzer Regiment 2*: 50 x Panzer IV, 26 x Panther
*SS-Sturmgeschütz Abteilung 2*: 41 x StuG III
*SS-Panzer Artillerie Regiment 2*: 12 x 105mm, 4 x 100mm, 4 x 15mm, 6 x Wespe, 5 x Hummel
*SS-Flak Abteilung 2*: 12 x 88mm, 9 x 37mm
*SS-Panzer Nachrichten Abteilung 2*
*SS-Panzer Aufklärungs Abteilung 2*: 4 companies

*SS-Panzer Pionier Abteilung 2*: three companies only
*Attached*
*SS-Werfer Abteilung 102*: 18 x Nebelwerfer
*II/Artillery Regiment 275*: 4 x 105mm, 4 x 100mm
*II/Artillery Regiment 191*: 9 x 75mm, 2 x 150mm
*Panzerjäger Abteilung 1041*: 15 x 88mm

## 17th SS Panzergrenadier Division *Götz von Berlichingen* (10 June)
(SS-Standartenführer Otto Baum)
Total strength: 17,321 men
*SS-Panzergrenadier Regiment 37*
*SS-Panzergrenadier Regiment 38*
*SS-Panzerjäger Abteilung 1*: 12 x Marder, 22 x Pak 40 (arrived later in the month)
*SS-Panzer Abteilung 17*: 42 x StuG III
*SS-Panzer Artillerie Regiment 17*: 25 x 105mm, 12 x 150mm, 4 x 100mm
*SS-Flak Abteilung 17*: 8 x 88mm, 9 x 37mm (arrived later in the month)
*SS-Panzer Nachrichten Abteilung 17*
*SS-Panzer Aufklärungs Abteilung 17*
*SS-Panzer Pionier Abteilung 17* (arrived later in the month)

# ARNHEM ORDER OF BATTLE

**II SS Panzer Corps Headquarters**
(SS-Obergruppenführer Willi Bittrich)
*SS-Arko II* (artillery command)
*SS-Corps Nachrichten Abteilung 400*

**9th SS Panzer Division** *Hohenstaufen*
(SS-Obersturmbannführer Walther Harzer)
*SS-Panzer Nachrichten Abteilung 9*, plus Military
Police, intelligence, escort troops, repair troops,
medical staff (280 men)
*SS-Panzergrenadier Regiment 19*: no heavy
weapons or APCs
*SS-Panzergrenadier Regiment 20*: no heavy
weapons or APCs

**Kampfgruppe** *Spindler*
(SS-Obersturmbannführer Ludwig Spindler)
*SS-Panzer Artillerie Regiment 9*: 120 men,
no guns
*SS-Panzer Regiment 9*: no tanks, 200–300 men
*SS-Panzerjäger Abteilung 9*: no heavy weapons,
2 x Pzjg IV, 2 x Pak 40, 2 x APC (120 men)

**Kampfgruppe** *von Allworden*
(SS-Hauptsturmführer Klaus von Allworden)

**Kampfgruppe** *Moeller*
(SS-Hauptsturmführer Hans Moeller)
*SS-Panzer Pionier Abteilung 9*: 90 men

**Kampfgruppe** *Gropp*
(SS-Untersturmführer Gropp)
*SS-Flak Abteilung 9*: 87 men, 1 x 88mm, 4 x
20mm
*SS Depot and Reserve Abteilung 16*: 440 men
(SS-Hauptsturmführer Sepp Kraft)
Total: 2500 men

**10th SS Panzer Division** *Frundsberg*
(SS-Brigadeführer Heinz Harmel)
*SS-Panzer Nachrichten Abteilung 10*
*SS-Panzergrenadier Regiment 21*: 1.5 battalions
*SS-Panzergrenadier Regiment 22*: 1 battalion plus
8 x Pak 40, 4 x SP 75mm AT
*SS-Panzer Artillerie Regiment 10*: 40 guns
*SS-Flak Abteilung 10*
*SS Training and Replacement Regiment 5*
*Kampfgruppe Brinkmann*
*SS-Panzer Aufklärungs Abteilung 10*

### NIJMEGEN DEFENCE
**Kampfgruppe** *Graebner*
*SS-Panzer Aufklärungs Abteilung 9*: 30 armoured
vehicles, 400 men
(SS-Hauptsturmführer Viktor Graebner)
*SS-Panzer Regiment 10*: 16 x Pz IV tanks
*SS-Panzer Pionier Abteilung 10*
(SS-Hauptsturmführer Albert Brandt)

**Kampfgruppe** *Reinhold*
tank crews as infantry
(SS-Hauptsturmführer Leo Hermann Reinhold)
*22 Panzergrenadier Regiment*, plus *3 Company,
21st Regiment*

**Kampfgruppe** *Euling*
100 men plus 4 x PzJg IV
(SS-Hauptsturmführer Karl Heinz Euling)

**Detached to Kampfgruppe** *Walther*
*Kampfgruppe Heinke*
*SS-Panzerjäger Abteilung 10*: 15 x PzJgr IV
*SS Kampfgruppe Seger*
*Artillery battery*: 6 x 105mm field guns, plus
infantry battalion from 9th SS Panzer Division
*SS Kampfgruppe Richter*
(SS-Hauptsturmführer Richter)

# ARDENNES ORDER OF BATTLE

### SIXTH PANZER ARMY
(SS-Oberstgruppenführer Josef "Sepp" Dietrich)

### I SS Panzer Corps *Leibstandarte Adolf Hitler*
(SS-Gruppenführer Hermann Priess)
SS-Arko I (artillery command)
SS-Corps Nachrichten Abteilung 101/501

### 1st SS Panzer Division *Leibstandarte Adolf Hitler*
(SS-Oberführer Wilhelm Mohnke)
Total strength: 22,000 men
SS-Panzer Nachrichten Abteilung "LSSAH" 1

### Kampfgruppe *Peiper*
(SS-Obersturmbannführer Jochen Peiper)
*SS-Panzer Regiment "LSSAH" 1*: 38 x Panther,
34 x Panzer IV
*SS-Panzer Abteilung 501*: 30 x Tiger II
*SS-Panzer Artillerie Regiment "LSSAH" 1,
II Abteilung*
*SS-Panzergrenadier Regiment 2 "LSSAH",
III Abteilung* (APC)

### Kampfgruppe *Hansen*
(SS-Standartenführer Max Hansen)
*SS-Panzergrenadier Regiment 1 "LSSAH"*:
6 x 150mm IG, 12 x 20mm
*SS-Panzerjäger Abteilung "LSSAH" 1*:
21 x PzJgr IV, 11 x Pak 40
*SS-Panzer Artillerie Regiment "LSSAH" 1,
I Abteilung*

### Kampfgruppe *Sandig*
(SS-Standartenführer Rudolf Sandig)
*SS-Panzergrenadier Regiment 2 "LSSAH"*:
6 x 150mm IG, 12 x 20mm
*SS-Flak Abteilung "LSSAH" 1*:
18 x 88mm, 18 x 37mm
*SS-Werfer Abteilung "LSSAH" 1*:
18 x 150mm, 6 x 210mm
*SS-Panzer Pionier Abteilung "LSSAH" 1*

*SS-Panzer-Artillerie-Regiment "LSSAH" 1,
III Abteilung*

### Kampfgruppe *Knittel*
(SS-Sturmbannführer Gustav Knittel)
*SS-Panzer Aufklärungs Abteilung "LSSAH" 1*

### 12th SS Panzer Division *Hitlerjugend*
(SS-Standartenführer Hugo Kraas)
Total strength: 22,000 men
*SS-Panzer Nachrichten Abteilung 12*

### Kampfgruppe *Kuhlmann*
(SS-Obersturmbannführer Herbert Kuhlmann)
*SS-Panzer Regiment 12*: 14 x Panther,
37 x Panzer IV
*506 Panzerjäger Abteilung* (Army):
28 x Jagdpanzer IV, 14 x Jagdpanther
*SS-Panzer Artillerie Regiment 12*: I Abteilung
*SS-Panzergrenadier Regiment 26*: III Abteilung

### Kampfgruppe *Muller*
(SS-Sturmbannführer Siegfried Muller)
*SS-Panzergrenadier Regiment 25*
*SS-Panzerjäger Abteilung 12*: 22 x Jagdpanzer IV
*SS-Panzer Artillerie Regiment 12*: II Abteilung

### Kampfgruppe *Krause*
(SS-Obersturmbannführer Bernard Krause)
*SS-Panzergrenadier Regiment 26*
*SS-Flak Abteilung 12*
*SS-Werfer Abteilung 12*
*SS-Panzer Pionier Abteilung 12*
*SS-Panzer Artillerie Regiment 12*: III Abteilung

### Kampfgruppe *Bremer*
(SS-Sturmbannführer Gerhardt Bremer)
*SS-Panzer Aufklärungs Abteilung 12*

## II SS Panzer Korps Headquarters

(SS-Obergruppenführer Willi Bittrich)
*SS-Arko II* (artillery command)
*SS-Corps Nachrichten Abteilung 400*

## 2nd SS Panzer Division *Das Reich*

Total strength: 18,000 men
(SS-Brigadeführer Heinz Lammerding)
*SS-Panzergrenadier Regiment 3 Deutschland*
*SS-Panzergrenadier Regiment Der Führer*
*SS-Infantry Regiment Langemarck*
*SS-Panzer Regiment 2*: 58 x Panther, 28 x Panzer
IV, 28 x StuG III
*SS-Panzerjäger Abteilung 2*: 20 x Jagdpanzer IV
*SS-Panzer Artillerie Regiment 2*
*SS-Flak Abteilung 2*
*SS-Panzer Nachrichten Abteilung 2*
*SS-Panzer Aufklärungs Abteilung 2*
*SS-Panzer Pioner Abteilung 2*
*Kampfgruppe Krag*
(SS-Sturmbannführer Ernst-August Krag)
*SS-Panzer Aufklärungs Abteilung 2*

## 9th SS Panzer Division *Hohenstaufen*

Total strength: 16,000 men
(SS-Oberführer Sylvester Stadler)
*SS-Panzergrenadier Regiment 19*
*SS-Panzergrenadier Regiment 20*
*SS-Panzer Regiment 9*
*I Abteilung*: 35 x Panther
*II Abteilung*: 28 x StuG III, 39 x Panzer IV
*SS-Panzerjäger Abteilung 9*: 21 x Jagdpanzer IV
*SS-Panzer Artillerie Regiment 9*
*SS-Flak Abteilung 9*
*SS-Panzer Nachrichten Abteilung 9*
*SS-Panzer Aufklärungs Abteilung 9*
*SS-Panzer Pioner Abteilung 9*
*519 schwer Panzerjäger Abteilung* (Army):
21 x Jagdpanther/StuG III

### KEY

**Abteilung** battalion
**APC** armoured personnel carrier
**Artillerie** artillery
**Aufklärungs** reconnaissance
**Ersatz** replacement
**Flak** antiaircraft
**IG** infantry gun
**Nachrichten** signals
**Nebelwerfer** rocket artillery
**Pak** antitank
**Panzerjäger** tank hunter
**Pioner** engineer
**schwer** heavy

| WAFFEN-SS OFFICER RANKS | | | |
|---|---|---|---|
| **Waffen-SS** | **German Army** | **British Army** | **US Army** |
| SS-Oberstgruppenführer | Generaloberst | General | General (5-star) |
| SS-Obergruppenführer | General | General | General (4-star) |
| SS-Gruppenführer | Generalleutnant | Lieutenant-General | Lieutenant-General (3-star) |
| SS-Brigadeführer | Generalmajor | Major-General | Major-General (2-star) |
| SS-Oberführer | – | Brigadier | Brigadier-General (1-star) |
| SS-Standartenführer | Oberst | Colonel | Colonel |
| SS-Obersturmbannführer | Oberstleutnant | Lieutenant-Colonel | Lieutenant-Colonel |
| SS-Sturmbannführer | Major | Major | Major |
| SS-Hauptsturmführer | Hauptmann | Captain | Captain |
| SS-Obersturmführer | Oberleutnant | Lieutenant | First Lieutenant |
| SS-Untersturmführer | Leutnant | Second Lieutenant | Second Lieutenant |

# BIBLIOGRAPHY

Badsey, Stephen, *Normandy 1944*, Opsrey, London, 1990

Bishop, Chris, *WWII: The Directory of Weapons*, Aerospace Publishing, London, 2000

Blumenson, Martin, *The Duel for France, 1944*, Da Capo Press, USA, 1963

Brett-Smith, Richard, *Hitler's Generals*, Osprey, London, 1976

Carrell, Paul, *Invasion – They're Coming!*, George Harrap, London, 1964

Cooper, Matthew and Lucas, James, *Panzer*, Macdonald, London, 1976

Cooper, Matthew and Lucas, James, *Panzergrenadier*, Macdonald and Jane's, London, 1977

Cooper, Matthew and Lucas, James, *Hitler's Elite*, Grafton, London, 1990

Delaforce, Patrick, *The Black Bull*, Chancellor Press, London, 2000

Downing, David, *The Devil's Virtuosos*, New English Library, London, 1976

Edwards, Roger, *Panzer: A Revolution in Warfare, 1939–45*, Arms and Armour, London, 1989

D'Este, Carlo, *A Genius For War*, HarperCollins, London 1996

Guderian, Heinz, *Panzer Leader*, Futura, London, 1979

Gudgin, Peter, *Armoured Firepower*, Sutton Publishing, Stroud, 1997

Forty, George, *German Tanks of World War Two*, Blandford Press, London, 1987

Hastings, Max, *Overlord*, Michael Joseph, London, 1984

Hastings, Max, *Das Reich*, Michael Joseph, London, 1981

Hitler, Adolf (trans Norman Cameron), *Hitler's Table Talk*, Weidenfeld & Nicolson, London, 1953

Irving, David, *The Trail of the Fox*, Weidenfeld & Nicolson, London, 1977

Jentz, Thomas, Doyle, Hilary and Sarson, Peter, *Tiger I*, Osprey, London, 1993

Jentz, Thomas, *Panzer Truppen*, Schiffer Military History, Atglen, 1996

Keegan, John, *Six Armies in Normandy*, Pimlico, London, 1982

Kershaw, Robert, *It Never Snows in September*, The Crowood Press, Marlborough, 1990

Kessler, Leo, *The Iron Fist*, Futura, London, 1977

Kleine, Egon and Kuhn, Volkmar, *Tiger*, Motorbuch Verlag, Stuttgart, 1990

Lefdevre, Eric, *Panzers in Normandy: Then and Now*, After the Battle, London, 1984

Lehman, Rudolf and Tieman Ralf, *The Leibstandarte IV/1*, J.J. Fedorowicz, Manitoba, 1993

MacDonald, Charles B., *The Battle of the Bulge*, Weidenfeld & Nicolson, London, 1984

McKee, Alexander, *Caen: Anvil of Victory*, Souvenir Press, London, 1964

Marshall, S.L.A., *Bastogne: The First Eight Days*, Center of US Military Hisory, US Army, Washington DC, 1996

Mellenthin, F.W., *Panzer Battles*, Futura, London, 1977

Meyer, Hubert, *Hitlerjugend*, J.J. Fedorowicz, Manitoba, 1994

Mitchell, Samuel, *Hitler's Legions*, Leo Cooper, London, 1985

Lord Montgomery of El Alamein, *Normandy to the Baltic*, Hutchinson, London, 1947

Pallud, Jean Paul, *Battle of the Bulge: Then and Now*, After the Battle, London, 1983

Quarrie, Bruce, *The Ardennes Offensive: Northern Sector*, Osprey, Oxford, 1999

Reynolds, Michael, *Steel Inferno*, Spellmount, Staplehurst, 1997

Reynolds, Michael, *Men of Steel*, Spellmount, Staplehurst, 1999

Ripley, Tim, *Steel Storm*, Sutton Publishing, Stroud, 2000

Rissik, David, *The DLI at War*, The Durham Light Infantry, Durham, 1952

Ryan, Cornelius, *A Bridge Too Far*, Hamish Hamiliton, 1974

Saunders, Tim, *Hill 112*, Leo Cooper, Barnsley, 2001

Sydnor, Charles, *Soldiers of Destruction: The SS Totenkopf Division 1933–45*, Princeton University Press, 1977

Trout, Ken, *Tank!*, Robert Hale, London, 1985

Wilmot, Chester, *Struggle for Europe*, Collins, London,1952

Zaloga, Steven, *Sherman*, Osprey, London, 1978

Zetterling, Niklas, *Normandy 1944*, J.J. Fedorowicz, Manitoba, 2000

Records of the Wehrmacht Inspector of Panzer Troops

War Diary of XXXXVIII Panzer Corps, December 1943

German Reports Series, 18 Volumes, US Army

*History of the Second World War*, Purnell & Sons, 1966–1974

# INDEX

## PICTURE CREDITS

*Ian Hogg:* 139

*Robert Hunt Library:* 17 (bottom), 18–19, 20, 21, 22 (both), 23, 24, 26 (both), 27 (both), 28, 29, 31, 33, 34 (both), 37, 39, 40–41, 42, 43 (both), 44, 46–47, 48 (bottom), 50, 51, 52 (top) 53, 56, 57, 58, 59, 60 (both), 61, 63, 67, 69, 70, 72 (bottom), 73, 74–75, 76, 77 (both), 78, 80, 81 (bottom), 82, 83, 88, 89, 90 (both), 96, 98, 99, 100, 104–105, 106–107, 113, 114, 115, 116, 117, 119, 120, 121, 124, 124–125, 126, 127, 128, 129, 130, 130–131, 133, 134, 135, 136–137, 140, 140–141, 144, 145, 147, 148, 149, 154, 155, 156, 161, 166, 167, 171, 172, 173, 174, 175, 176, 177, 178–179, 180, 181, 182, 183, 185, 186–187, 190–191, 191, 196, 197, 198–199, 201, 202–203, 204, 205, 209, 210, 211, 213

*Private collection:* 32, 35, 49, 102, 106, 192–193, 194

*Tim Ripley:* 13 (both), 14, 15, 16, 17 (top)

*Antony Shaw:* 158

*TRH Pictures:* 10–11, 12, 25, 30, 36, 38, 48 (top), 52 (bottom), 64–65, 66, 72 (top), 81 (top), 84, 85, 91, 92–93, 94 (both), 95, 101, 103, 109, 110, 111, 118, 122–123, 142–143, 146–147, 150–151, 157, 159, 160–161, 162–163, 164, 164–165, 168–169, 187, 195, 200, 206–207